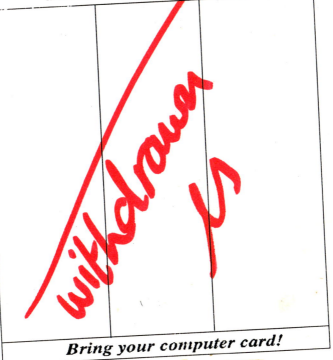

Mike Procter
and Cricket

Mike Procter
and Cricket

PELHAM BOOKS

Printed in Great Britain by
PELHAM BOOKS LTD
44 Bedford Square
London WC1B 3DU
1981

ISBN 0 7207 1326 9

Set in Great Britain by
Saildean Limited,
Walton on Thames.
Printed and bound in Great Britain
by Billing and Sons Limited
Guildford, London, Oxford, Worcester

Contents

Preface

Many readers of this book will strain for various implications behind my views on politics and sport. That's why politics is dealt with in the first chapter; I trust my opinions on this thorny and anguishing topic are clear and that the reader will then be able to concentrate on cricket for the rest of the book.

As a jet-age cricketer, playing the game all the year round, I don't need to stress how grateful I am to the sport. Because I was lucky enough to possess some talent at cricket, I've travelled the world, broadened my horizons, learnt a lot about life and met some wonderful people. I don't know how I would have coped with being cooped up in an office instead of pursuing the outdoor life. When the time comes to retire, I shall have no regrets, merely a sadness that a deeply satisfying and exciting period of my life has ended.

If I named everyone who's had a beneficial effect on my life and career, the list would fill this book. All I can say is that I'm eternally grateful to so many friends, relatives and players for their many kindnesses. My thanks also to Pat Murphy for collaborating with me in this book and for fitting in with my usual chaotic schedule.

MIKE PROCTER

Mike Procter in Cricket

Born 15 September 1946

1961–4	Played for Natal Schools XI
1962–3	South African Schools XI
1963	Vice-Captain of South African Schools touring team in England
1965	Debut in first-class cricket: for Gloucestershire *v.* South African Tourists
1965–6	Debut for Natal
1966–7	Test debut *v.* Australia
1968	Joined Gloucestershire staff
1969–70	Played four Tests *v.* Australia and made debut for Western Province
1970	Played for Rest of the World side in five 'Tests' in England
1970–71	Debut for Rhodesia. Appointed National Coach
1971–72	Appointed captain of Rhodesia
1976–77	Rejoined Natal
1977	Appointed Gloucestershire captain
1977	Joined World Series Cricket on three-year contract
1977–79	Played WSC in Australia

1

Cricket and Politics

Not until I played professional cricket in England did I realise that the black man wasn't inferior to me. I was brought up in a typically middle-class South African environment and you just didn't question the laws of the land. In my naïveté, I assumed apartheid was correct, because it was there.

When I first came to England, I couldn't get over the sight of white men sweeping the streets and doing other menial tasks. I'd always assumed that was the lot of the black man. Quite simply, I'd been brainwashed. But my eyes were opened when I started playing with and against decent, civilised men like Clive Lloyd, Basil D'Oliveira, Gary Sobers and John Shepherd. They opened my eyes about racial discrimination and made me realise how blinkered my attitude had been.

That was a long time ago and I'm glad to say that later generations of young South African sportsmen don't have the same rigid attitude. I can't think of any white South African cricketer who wouldn't play with or against non-whites now, and that's an attitude which I believe is held by the overwhelming majority in the Republic. We only care about ability on the sports field and we genuinely want the non-whites to have the same chance of success. Having said that, I appreciate that you can't change the laws of the land overnight; I abhor the system of apartheid as much as anyone and I think it's totally wrong that a black man can compete on equal terms with me on a cricket field, drink with me afterwards and then has to travel home in a non-whites railway compartment. But changes are coming in South Africa and I hope equality of opportunity will soon be established. However, changes can't come overnight in any society, least of all South African. They have to be gradual and peaceful.

There's no doubt in my mind that isolating South Africa from international sport in the last decade has helped break down the barriers to segregated sport in my country. By South Africa's standards, the changes have been dramatic in recent years – for example, any non-white can play with or against any white man in most sports, something that would have been unheard of not so long ago. I suppose we had no option really. We had to change our ways or be isolated from international sport for good. But now I think it's time to bring us back into the international fold; we've done so much in recent years that it would be nice to get some encouragement and recognition of our progress from other countries. My eyes were opened by contact with other non-white sportsmen and the same thing applied to men like Eddie Barlow, the Pollock brothers, Hylton Ackerman and Barry Richards. Our experiences proved that total isolation doesn't work over a long period. You can only break down barriers by dialogue – that's why I was pleased that the British Lions came to the Republic in 1980. I know it looked as if they were giving the seal of approval to the apartheid regime but if they took the opportunity to hammer home the gospel of non-racial sport to high-ranking rugby and Government officials, they will have done a good job.

Rugby is the real god in South Africa, not cricket; it's

tied up with the Afrikaaner philosophy, and the heartland of apartheid and the Nationalist Government is in the rugby-mad areas of Orange Free State and Northern Transvaal. Get through to them and you'll indeed make progress towards dismantling apartheid in our society, not just in sport. A lot of fuss was made about the Lions tour in 1974, when the anti-apartheid people again said they were sanctioning that system. They couldn't have been more wrong – I think that was a really telling blow to the system. Our heavy defeat meant we were no longer invincible and the theory of white supremacy took a real hammer blow. Willie John McBride's great team did more to develop cracks in the wall of apartheid than years of argument and demonstrations.

If the Government officially made the Springbok Rugby side multiracial, the barriers would come tumbling down all over the place. But that will take time, something we seem to be desperately short of. Great progress is being made in the world of rugby, but we must beware of window-dressing. There's no point in selecting non-white players who just aren't good enough, they'll feel patronised and inferior and retreat into their shells. In cricket, there aren't enough good non-white players yet to challenge a white man for the same place. If a Test team was selected tomorrow all eleven places would be filled by whites, on merit. That's because facilities for non-whites are still generally poor; I've been to a number of Indian schools in Durban and their cricket facilities are practically non-existent. As director of coaching for Natal, I have to organise nets and provide the best facilities for cricketers of any colour, but it's disappointing to see how few non-whites come along. That's partly due to a sort of apartheid system in reverse where some of the non-white children coached by me get banned from their school sides because they've mixed with whites in my nets. It's all very sad.

13

Where are the top-class non-white cricketers? Well, Omar Henry is a good left-arm spinner who's played several times for Eddie Barlow's Western Province side, Babboo Abraham is another in the same mould who's played on and off for my team, Natal, but there aren't many of proven class. That's not their fault, the system is still wrong. I remember two black South Africans playing in the first Datsun double wicket competition at the Wanderers Ground in 1973. Edward Habane and Edmund Ntitincka earned as much in two days cricket as they normally would in a year. They played against the top players from Pakistan, New Zealand, Australia and South Africa – then it was back to their poor facilities and apartheid for another year. I felt sorry for these great blokes, they were victims of a situation that was out of their control. The same thing would have applied to John Shepherd and Younis Ahmed. They toured South Africa with the Derrick Robins side in the early seventies and they were regarded as honorary whites for the tour. But if they'd come back a month later as private citizens, they would be classified non-white. Anomalies like that are difficult to defend.

It would be an insult to non-whites if we packed our Currie Cup sides with them. It may impress the outside world but we would all know it was mere window-dressing. We have to work hard at organising a system that helps non-whites get as good a start as I got in my cricketing career. I'm afraid merit selection should mean just that.

It is difficult to know what else we sportsmen can do about a situation that is fundamentally political. I was heavily involved in the famous walk-off at Newlands in 1971 as a protest against the Nationalist Government's refusal to permit integrated cricket, and we were regarded as extreme and dangerous by the Afrikaaner press. It's ironic really; our public plea for moderation and decency

14

was regarded by the Government as subversive because it challenged tradition.

That walk-off at Newlands was a proud day for those cricketers involved. Once and for all, we'd shown where we stood in relation to apartheid in sport. Events had come to a head because the Springbok tour of Australia was due within a year and there were rumours that it would be called off. In an effort to save the trip, the South African Cricket Association asked the Government if two blacks could be included in the tour party. Sounds naïve and it smacks off window-dressing, I agree, but at the time SACA's motives were well-intentioned. In the event, the Government refused and the news leaked out on the eve of a final trial for those likely to be selected. Transvaal, the Currie Cup champions, were due to play the Rest of South Africa and as we gathered at Newlands the attitude of the Government was the major talking point. Over dinner that night, I discussed it with Eddie Barlow, Dennis Lindsay, Barry Richards and Graeme and Peter Pollock. We felt something should be done to support SACA's initiative publicly. Our initial reaction was to refuse to play in the forthcoming match. Now the respected radio commentator Charles Fortune was staying in the same hotel and we asked his opinion. He pointed out that a refusal to play would upset those whose support we wanted; the best thing would be to walk off at some suitably dramatic moment in the game and resume play a few minutes later. That way, the spectators wouldn't be harmed and both SACA and the Government would then know where we stood.

We decided to put the plan to both sets of players the following morning. The rest of South Africa side were all for it and the Transvaal players voted seven to four in favour. We then decided to draft a press statement and agreed that nobody would comment afterwards. The team managers and the umpires were put in the picture and as I walked out that morning on to the Newlands pitch, I was conscious we were taking part in a piece of sporting history. We knew what we were doing. At various stages we'd all said that cricket should be mixed in South Africa – an opinion frowned on by our Government – but now we were united in saying this publicly. It was a serious occasion and there were none of the usual sarcastic comments and wisecracks as we took the field.

I bowled the first ball of the match to Barry Richards, who was guesting for Transvaal; he pushed a single to the off side and we all walked off the field. The openers left their bats on the pitch, the umpires stayed there and the players trooped into the dressing-room as the statement was handed in to the press box. It read: 'We cricketers feel that the time has come for an expression of our views. We fully support the South African Cricket Association's application to include non-whites on the tour to Australia if good enough and furthermore, subscribe to merit being the only criterion on the cricket field.'

Of course there was a fair old furore among sports officials, pressure groups, Cabinet Ministers and other politicians as the news reverberated around the world. We players seemed somehow aloof from it all; we'd said our piece, taken our stand and quickly resumed the match. We didn't think we were being unpatriotic, we simply felt that the principle of merit selection was vital to ensure South Africa's sporting future. Subsequently the Australian tour was called off but I feel the Newlands walk-off did a hell of a lot. From now on, white cricketers didn't have to look over their shoulders when agreeing that there was nothing wrong with mixed cricket. We'd put the ball in the politician's court and the fact that there's been so much relaxation of 'petty' apartheid rules proves that we didn't harden the Government's attitudes, even though there was no immediate reaction from the Government. Now there is integrated, multiracial cricket in most parts of South Africa. Would that have come as soon without the Newlands walk-off?

I blame the politicians for much of South Africa's problems in sport. They're always saying that politics shouldn't be brought into sport, yet they did just that during the D'Oliveira affair in 1968 which led to our isolation. I agree, it all looked a little fishy when Dolly was originally dropped from the tour party for South Africa, then reinstated when Tom Cartwright dropped out through injury. But all cricketers know that selectors do some funny things at times and for better or worse, they are the ones who should have the final say on whether a man is good enough to tour. But the politicians got involved and the rest is history.

Anybody who says politics and sport shouldn't mix is being naïve. I'm afraid that happens all over the world – look at the Olympics in Moscow and the fuss Mrs Thatcher, the British Prime Minister, made in trying to dissuade the Lions from going to South Africa that same year. There was the time when Barry Richards and I were all set to fly out to India in 1974 for a charity match to aid flood victims. The Indian Government refused us entry, even though we'd played county cricket with some of the Indians, and even though we were getting no profits from the trip. Barry and I really thought we could do something for relations between our country and India, yet our motives were misunderstood. I remember another baffling occasion, in 1977 when I skippered a Rest of the World side at Arundel against the Australians. Three Pakistanis were in my side: Sadiq Mohammad, his brother Mushtaq and Zaheer Abbas. Throughout the day all three were being called to the telephone and finally I asked Zaheer what was going on. Zaheer said the calls had come from top-ranking officials back home, saying that the three Pakistanis shouldn't have been playing under a South African, even though two of

17

them had been in the Gloucestershire side with me for years!

When I was national coach in Rhodesia in the early 1970s, I always used to invite top players from the West Indies, Pakistan and India to Salisbury for a double wicket competition. Those players all wanted to come but every time their governments refused permission. It makes me so angry! What's wrong with playing cricket, making new friends and trying to heal old wounds?

So many things have frustrated us in our attempts to get South African sport on a proper mixed basis. There's the attitude of Hassan Howa for a start. Now I admire Mr Howa for the consistent policy he's followed throughout the years. 'No normal sport in an abnormal society,' he vows, and as president of the South African Board of Control he's obviously got a lot of power. SACBOC controls Coloured and Indian cricket in South Africa and Mr Howa has steadfastly refused to join with the South African Cricket Association to organise mixed cricket on a proper footing. If all the bodies joined together and presented a united front to the Government, I feel progress would be even greater off the sports field, but Mr Howa remains aloof from it all. He says that white cricketers didn't give a thought to non-whites until isolation, and he may well be right about that. But we've all spoken up now for the cause of mixed cricket and we're all looking for more and more concessions on and off the sports field. But Mr Howa has acted regularly like a politician, rather than a cricket administrator; he thought SACA's attempt to get two blacks on the trip to South Africa was just a bluff and then he turned down a SACA grant of 50,000 Rand because he suspected the motives. Just think what all that money could have done for the poor facilities of non-white cricketers! Then there was the incredible ban on a Coloured player just for watching a cricket game. Dickie Conrad went along to Newlands to watch Western Province play the Derrick Robbins side that contained a few non-whites, and Mr Howa then banned him from all games under the jurisdiction of his organisation! There's been pettiness on all sides, though. It was wrong of the Government to refuse a passport to Mr Howa so he could attend cricket meetings outside South Africa. There was the time in 1974 when I wanted to bring a Rest of the World side over to South Africa. It would be drawn from all countries and I thought it would be great for the Test-starved Republic, as well as another way of breaking down rigid barriers. I was even prepared to make a loss on the venture. But, with plans well in advance, my scheme was turned down by the South African Cricket Association for the ludicrous reason that they feared the South African team would be thrashed inside a couple of days. The feeling was that our players would be short of practice, while the Rest of the World side would be coming straight from competitive matches. I thought that was rubbish; the South African side may not have been as impressive as a few years previously, but they would have trained hard for the match. It would have done the image of my country a lot of good and the non-whites would have enjoyed seeing their heroes competing on equal terms with white cricketers.

SACA also acted disastrously in my opinion when they vetoed a mixed tour of South Africa in 1971. The idea was that an England Eleven – including Basil D'Oliveira – would tour for a month in March 1972. It was the brain child of two young South African newspapermen, Gert Wolmarans and Hennie Viljoen. They organised a sponsor and worked out a five-match itinerary, involving a one-day limited overs match and four unofficial 'Tests', and they even managed to get Government permission for D'Oliveira to make the trip. Barry Richards and I were

19

quickly sold on the idea and we persuaded Dolly to agree. It was all very secretive but players like Ray Illingworth, Tony Greig, Alan Knott, Fred Titmus and John Snow were all lined up for the tour.

Everything was set up – then SACA pulled the rug from under our feet. The late Jack Cheetham, the SACA President, refused to sanction the scheme, something we never even thought was possible. I still can't imagine why SACA vetoed the trip; we weren't trying to usurp their authority, we weren't out to make fat profits, because all of it would have been handed over to SACA to help develop non-white cricket. It was one of the biggest disappointments of my life and it seemed so unnecessary. The cause of mixed cricket was delayed another eighteen months until Younis Ahmed and John Shepherd played in the Datsun double-wicket contest; Basil D'Oliveira would have been the first black man to play at the Wanderers ground and after all the trauma he'd endured, he deserved that. After all these years, I'm still angry about it.

The last decade has been full of frustrations like that for South Africa's cricketers. I realise we won't get too much sympathy from certain sections of society for that state-ment, but I think I'm entitled to ask, just what do we have to do to get back into Test cricket? When the International Cricket Conference kicked us out of the Test arena, I suppose we all knew it was bound to come. But the ICC did leave us with tasks to perform before we could claim our place back. Today those conditions are fulfilled, indeed they have been for several years: cricket in South Africa is totally integrated from club to national level. Merit selection exists all the way down to school level and many blacks hold administrative posts. The ICC seems to applaud our strides secretly, but won't do all that much for us. In 1979 a delegation representing thirteen of the twenty ICC countries found that our cricket was non-racial, yet the ICC was noncommittal about our progress after its annual meeting that year.

My own feeling is that South Africa won't get back into Test Cricket for some years to come, if ever. Certain countries in the ICC – India, Pakistan, and the West Indies – just won't budge from their standpoint of 'no normal sport in an abnormal society' and there is deadlock among the pro and anti-South Africa factions. One possible result would be if the black countries simply played against themselves while Australia, New Zealand and South Africa did the same at Test level. But that would be very unsatisfactory and would dilute the impact of Test cricket. I think the South African cricket administrators have done all in their power to get us back into the Test arena but their efforts clearly won't impress certain influential people, who seem to forget there are subtle forms of apartheid practised all over the world. What about Australia? A black man isn't allowed to go over there and settle next door to the whites. Our critics forget that it takes time to dismantle a system that, however wrong, has been in existence for a very long time. Sport has done much in recent years to break down those barriers, but sportsmen can't change the laws overnight. I can't see how South Africa can have 'one man, one vote' overnight, because that would leave the Bantus running the country and the Indians and the Coloureds wouldn't stand for that. It's a hell of a complex problem to solve but I am convinced of one thing: recognition by the ICC of our efforts towards mixed cricket would hasten the progress towards a totally integrated society.

South Africans are not complacent about the changes in the past few years. For myself, I don't feel guilty about my tacit acceptance of the present apartheid set-up. As a boy I was blinkered and I needed travel to broaden my perceptions, but I feel I've done a fair amount towards integrated sport in the last decade. There's only so much a

21

sportsman can do, after all. A man like Basil D'Oliveira has done more than anybody; he behaved incredibly in 1968 in the face of terrible pressure. In his own way, Basil did so much for the dignity of the black man. He opened many a pair of jaundiced eyes by proving he was as good as any of us, on and off the field.

I don't feel bitter about being banned from Test cricket. When it first happened I thought it would just be a short, sharp dose of isolation, but the years have dragged on and I've come to terms with it. There's no point in eating my heart out and at least I've tasted Test cricket as a young man, and also World Series Cricket in 1977/79. I feel more sorry for younger men like Allan Lamb and Peter Kirsten, who must be very frustrated after proving themselves in the pressure cooker of English county cricket. And isolation has been harder on men like Ali Bacher, Dennis Lindsay and the Pollock brothers, because they haven't been playing county cricket. For them, playing in the Currie Cup was the highest thing they could aim for; the build-up to these matches is now very intense and when I played in Rhodesia, any games against South African Provinces had as much tension as some Test matches, because it was the most competitive brand of cricket available to some of us. Since isolation, the game's a lot harder in South Africa – there's a lot more needle and controversy flying around and indeed in 1973/4 there was talk of getting all the Currie Cup captains round the table in a bid to clean up the game. That was going a bit too far but there's no doubt that isolation has meant we all try that much harder in our rare first-class matches in South Africa.

The only way out of this professional frustration at the moment is for young South Africans to try to get qualified for other Test countries. Kepler Wessels is doing that by living in Australia, while Allan Lamb and Chris Smith are thinking of doing the same for England. I got involved in negotiations with Lord's about my status at the end of the 1980 season in England and the press read far too much into it.

Gloucestershire wanted me to be registered 'available for England' because it had been made clear that all the counties were having to cut down on the amount of overseas players allowed to play in any one game. We have three at Bristol – myself and the two Pakistanis, Sadiq and Zaheer – so my county applied for me to be judged an Englishman in the context of limiting overseas players. The press jumped to all sorts of conclusions – 'Procter for England?' said the headlines – and although it's true that the Lord's ruling means I'm now available for England, I'm sure that will never happen. For a start, I'm too old, my bowling isn't quick enough any longer and I'm carrying a few injuries. But fundamentally I'm a South African, and in my heart of hearts it would be wrong for me to play Test cricket for a country other than my own. Despite my criticisms of my country, I'm still proud to be a South African; I still want to be a citizen of South Africa, and my son Gregg is now being educated full-time over there. When my career in English cricket is over, I shall return to South Africa for good, so how could I play for England? I've had my thrills in Test cricket, whereas South African-born players like Tony Greig and Basil D'Oliveira didn't get that chance, so I didn't blame them for qualifying for England.

I managed to get into county cricket because of my Test performances for my country, so it would be wrong to line my pockets on the strength of those deeds more than a decade ago. It would have been different if I'd been a naturalised British subject from 1970, but it would be totally wrong for me to deny a place in the English team to someone better qualified. I didn't duck the question when it was put to me at the Lord's meeting, and when I answered it truthfully, I thought, 'Well, that's blown it.' But I like to think they took into account my strong links with Gloucestershire over the years and they gave a decision that surprised me, but was great for my county. They gave me a very fair hearing and I was delighted by their ruling, but the fact remains that the only country I shall ever play Test cricket for will be South Africa. Yet somehow I doubt if Mike Procter has a Test Match future ...

2

Test Cricket

My first taste of Test cricket came in the Oval Test match of 1966 when England beat the West Indies by an innings. I was, of all things, a dressing-room attendant for the tourists in that match. Barry Richards, Lee Irvine and myself had been on a tour to England with a Wilfred Isaacs XI and we decided to stay on in London when it ended. We had hardly any cash, and we were hungry and our financial problems came to a head during the Oval Test. So we walked up to the Surrey secretary and asked for odd jobs. We were lucky; we cleaned the pads and boots of men like Gary Sobers, Wes Hall and Rohan Kanhai and got a terrific view of the Test from their dressing-room. I remember elegant hundreds by Tom Graveney and John Murray, Brian Close catching Sobers for nought in the bat pad position, the great bowling of John Snow and his long last-wicket partnership with Ken Higgs. It gave me the taste for Test cricket and Barry and Lee felt the same. A few months later, the Australians were due in South Africa to play five Tests and we set our sights on playing for our country.

I was the only one of the trio lucky enough to get the call in that series. For some reason that I still can't explain, I emerged as a fast bowler that season. In the previous season (my first) I'd only taken seventeen wickets but now everything fell into place. Perhaps cleaning all those boots at the Oval toughened me up! I hardly seemed to notice that my batting had fallen away, because my sights were set on that first Springbok cap and I didn't care how I got in the side. I was twelfth man in the first two Tests and I was disappointed. South Africa was recovering its esteem in Test cricket – we'd beaten England in 1965 in their own country – and I wanted to be part of it all. After all, I was twenty, and in South Africa that's not considered all that young for sporting prowess at international level. In that first Test, I watched the great Graeme Pollock hit his first ball for six and Dennis Lindsay hook the Aussie fast bowlers out of sight for a superb 182, and enjoyed watching our batsmen grind them into the dust for a second innings total of 620. They were left to get 495 to win, and on the last day I managed to set foot on the field and play a small part in our first Test win in our own country against Australia. I caught Graham McKenzie and Neil Hawke off Trevor Goddard's bowling and the crowd went wild as we stormed home winners by 233 runs. But my debut as substitute fielder was tinged with sadness. I replaced the great Colin Bland, who injured a knee chasing a ball round the boundary's edge. He never played Test cricket after that and his brilliant fielding was never the same again.

The next Test was an anticlimax and I watched frustrated as the Aussies beat us by six wickets after we'd followed on. Graeme Pollock's 209 after pulling a thigh muscle will linger long in my memory, as will McKenzie's ability to dig the ball in at our batsmen from a placid Newlands wicket. But Simpson and Stackpole's centuries set up the Australians and we were always in second place.

By this time I was fretting; surely the selectors will give me a chance now? After all, we'd just lost a Test and they're bound to change the side, aren't they? They did, and on 20 January 1967 I went out to bat for my country on my home ground at Durban. Our score was 90 for 5 and I didn't help our cause that much. I was petrified with nerves and it wasn't until I got back to the pavilion – bowled for one – that I realised just what had been happening. But the next day I made up for it with the ball, and I can still see my first Test wicket, just before midday on the second morning. Bobby Simpson got a faint off-side edge and Dennis Lindsay did the rest behind the stumps. I took 3 for 27, they had to follow on and I then took 4 for 71 in the second innings. At lunch my figures had read 0/46, so I was pleased with the final analysis. So we strolled home by eight wickets and for a young man called Procter, it was a deeply satisfying moment. I felt proud for myself, of course, but also for my family and friends for all the encouragement and advice they'd given me. I still couldn't believe that just over a year ago I hadn't even played in first-class cricket, nor could I work out how a batsman could take seven wickets in his debut Test against the Aussies!

In fact, my batting was pretty dreadful thoughout that series (I made 17 runs in three innings) but I made up for that with the ball. In the fourth Test at Johannesburg (a rain-affected draw) I picked up another six wickets, one of them proving to be the most satisfying piece of bowling so far in my career. Bill Lawry thought the ball was passing just outside the off-stump and he let it go. To his astonishment, the ball nipped back and hit the top of his off-stump. I'll never forget the roar of the crowd as Lawry dragged himself away from the crease. It was one of the best deliveries I've ever bowled.

So to the fifth Test and an easy seven wicket win for us, but not before I'd been dismissed for nought in the most embarrassing circumstances – hit wicket after ducking under what I thought was going to be a bouncer from

McKenzie. But Pollock scored another brilliant hundred and we wound up the series 3–1 winners. There was no doubt in the minds of South African cricketers that we were entering a golden age.

I can remember almost everything about that series: the amazing batting of Dennis Lindsay, which brought him two centuries; the genius of Pollock; the shrewd, nagging, medium-pace bowling of Trevor Goddard; the uncomplaining hard work of Graham McKenzie; and the neat, stylish batting of Bobby Simpson and Ian Redpath. To this cricket-mad youngster, it only seemed yesterday that I'd sat day-dreaming in class at school, picking my World Eleven to play South Africa. Yet here I was with 15 wickets at a cost of 17 each in my first three Tests! I didn't care that my batting looked amateurish, that would sort itself out, I hoped. The main point was that I was in the Springbok side alongside some great players, and I hadn't disgraced myself.

There's no doubt the Aussies missed Doug Walters, who'd started sensationally against England the previous year; but he'd been called up by the army. Perhaps they should have picked Norman O'Neill and Brian Booth to bolster up their middle order batting but, as usual, the Australian selectors had given youth its chance and who can blame them? South Africa has always had the same philosophy. Unfortunately, Simpson's side dropped too many catches throughout the tour and they never had any real support for the magnificent McKenzie. And their tactics with Lindsay were all wrong – in the second Test, they got him caught and bowled cheaply when he misjudged a hook and the ball bounded from his face. Thereafter the Aussies thought Dennis would be vulnerable to the short-pitched ball, but he kept hooking and pulling them out of sight. They should have bowled just outside his off-stump, where he was nowhere near as effective. I well remember his century at Johannesburg in the fourth Test – he got it in 107 minutes in a brilliant display of hooking that included four sixes. The Aussies just had a mental block about Dennis and when you consider that he also took twenty-four catches behind the stumps in the series, it's safe to say he was a dominant influence.

Everything in the Springbok garden was looking rosy by February 1967. Young players like Barry Richards, Lee Irvine and Hylton Ackerman were knocking on the door of the Test team and we had beaten England and Australia inside eighteen months. Next stop, the home series against England in 1968/9. Or so we thought. The d'Oliveira Affair changed all that and sparked off a chain of circumstances that led to our ban from Tests. For three years we had to kick our heels, desperate to flex our international muscles. Then the Australians, en route from a tour of Ceylon and India, agreed to stop over and play four Tests. The news was greeted deliriously in South Africa, and although we showed our appreciation to our visitors off the field, there was no mercy when the cricket started. We won all four Tests, and although the Aussies were no doubt fatigued after the tour of India, we would have triumphed whatever the circumstances. It was un-questionably the finest side I've ever played in – our batting was long and prolific, Peter Pollock and I took 41 wickets between us (more than half the Aussie wickets to fall) and our fielding was brilliant.

On paper, Bill Lawry's side was a better one than Bobby Simpson's in 1966/7. The captain, Stackpole, Ian Chappell and Redpath were experienced players at Test level, Walters was back from his military duties, Paul Sheahan looked a fine batsman, Alan Connolly was sure to support McKenzie with the new ball and Johnny Gleeson and Ashley Mallett were high-class spinners. But again their catching let them down, their batting crumbled

29

against quick bowling and poor McKenzie had a nightmare tour. He took just one wicket for 331 runs in three Tests and overwork meant he was just a shadow of his former superb self.

In the first Test at Newlands, steady batting all the way down the order, plus dynamic bowling from Peter Pollock were enough to see us home by a margin of 170 runs. Our winning margin at Durban in the following Test was more complete: an innings and 129 runs inside four days. We made 622 for 9 declared after Graeme Pollock and Barry Richards had played two of the finest innings I've ever seen. Barry, in his second Test, scored 94 before lunch and in an hour afterwards, he and Graeme added 102 runs of sheer class. Richards stroked the ball all over the field, while Graeme simply stood up and smashed the bowlers. Not that Connolly, Gleeson and Co. bowled badly. You had to feel sorry for them shaping up to sheer genius at each end. Graeme ended up with 274, the highest score in Tests by a South African, and he'd murdered the bowling with incredible power.

The third Test at Johannesburg was another comfortable win, by 307 runs, and it was made doubly significant by the last wicket in the match being taken by Trevor Goddard, who planned to retire from first-class cricket at the end of the game. A great way to end a superb all-round career. This was our sixth win in the last eight Tests over the Aussies and we kept thinking – surely they're going to turn the tables on us shortly? They didn't ... they went down by 323 runs as their batsmen again crumpled. Barry Richards got another masterful century. Lee Irvine made his maiden Test century, I took 6 for 73 in the second innings, so it was a pretty good Test for those three blokes who'd cleaned the West Indians' boots a few years back at the Oval!

I was particularly pleased with my bowling in that second knock because I was running a high temperature.

But I had to bowl because my opening partner, Peter Pollock had pulled a hamstring and could not bowl. In that series I bowled as quick as at any stage in my career, taking 26 wickets. To those who say I've bowled fast in English county cricket, I say: 'You should have seen me against Bill Lawry's side.' Everything seemed to click, I was fit and strong, my opening partner Peter Pollock was a great help to me, and my fielders backed me up brilliantly. Eddie Barlow's fielding in the slips is a vivid memory from that series, he took eight catches, some of them absolute blinders, and, to my knowledge, he didn't drop one in four Tests. He also scored two centuries and picked up several valuable wickets at crucial stages. His was a great all-round effort.

The Australian batsmen disappointed me. Stackpole just couldn't resist trying to hook and cut the fast bowlers and he was caught at first slip or behind the wicket six times in his eight Test innings. Walters seemed to have a technique all of his own against pace; he hopped all around the place trying to avoid the short-pitched delivery. The Aussies never managed a single century partnership in the series and Ian Chappell was their biggest disappointment. Before the series started, his captain said he was the best batsman in the world on all wickets and that might have worried Chappell, because lavish praise like that is hard to live up to. In the end he only got 92 runs against us in eight knocks and he managed to get out in the most unlucky ways – in the first Test he hooked a bouncer from Pollock straight at Lee Irvine at leg slip, he knocked it up and the other close fielder caught it.

That was the start of a terrible run for Chappell. He was caught down the leg side by the keeper, on another occasion off the back of the bat when he'd finished the shot and Eddie Barlow got him first ball with a beauty in the third Test. I'm sure that series scarred Chappell for a time and toughened him up. He emerged a fine captain, a world-class bat, and he made sure nobody could ever feel sorry for him again. On that tour of South Africa, he didn't have the best of relationships with his captain. Too often, Lawry would retreat into his shell and appear moody and irritable while Chappell would try to get the team into a cohesive unit by acting as peacemaker. He was vice-captain, after all, but the idea of Chappell playing the diplomat is an amusing one, considering his outbursts of recent years!

One Australian particularly impressed me in this series. Johnny Gleeson was a high-class spinner and none of us could really fathom which way the ball would turn. We all had our theories, of course, but by the end of the series only Barry Richards – a law unto himself anyway – could honestly claim to have worked it all out satisfactorily. I tried to get as near as possible to the pitch of the ball and pick up the direction of the spin through the air, but it wasn't an infallible method. Gleeson remains the spinner I've had most trouble with throughout my career.

On 10 March 1970 the curtain rang down on South Africa's Test history for the time being. When Ali Bacher, our captain, caught Alan Connolly off Pat Trimborn's bowling, we completed a memorable thrashing of Bill Lawry's side. Since that day, no country has officially wanted to play Tests against us and a fine South African team has simply festered. The huge margins of victory in that 1969/70 series surely proved the point that we were, at that time, the best national side in the world. True, some ICC members didn't want to play us, but the West Indies were in decline, and India and Pakistan were both going through a formative process. But with cricket interest and quality at its highest-ever level in South Africa, we suddenly had no teams to play against. We were due to tour England in a couple of months but there was never any chance of that. The anti-apartheid demonstrators, with their sophisticated means of disruption, would have ensured that the tour would have been a nightmare. Cricket is an easy game to disrupt and the massive security precautions meant the tour would not be a financial proposition. We could hardly blame the MCC for yielding to the Prime Minister's request to cancel the tour because of the threat to public order. Isolation was beginning and although we had fond hopes of going to Australia in a further eighteen months' time, I didn't feel very optimistic.

The hardened attitudes of the politicians were always on hand to frustrate the ideals of the sportsmen. It's ironic to reflect that the wrong sport was disrupted. It shouldn't have been cricket, the game beloved of South Africans of English extraction. Rugby is the sport of the Afrikaaners and they keep the Nationalist Government in power. Most Afrikaaners don't care that much for cricket while rugby, with few exceptions, has continued its international course in South Africa. After all, not many black countries play rugby union to international standard.

The record books say I played just seven Tests but I will always maintain the figure was twelve. A Rest of the World side was hastily organised to fill in the gap left by the cancelled South African visit to England in 1970 and we agreed to play five international matches as well. At the time, they were regarded by *Wisden,* the bible of cricket, as official Tests and I can assure you they were played in just that spirit. But recently *Wisden* has seen fit to rob those five matches of their Test status; don't ask me why, because records have never been my forté but it does seem unfair that a fine player like Glamorgan's Alan Jones should be robbed of his solitary England cap years after he'd played in what was an authentic Test to all the players.

That series was a rewarding and enjoyable experience

33

and one in the eye for those cynics who thought there might be discord in our dressing-room. South Africans Barlow, Procter, Richards and the two Pollocks mixed easily with West Indians Sobers, Kanhai, Lloyd and the Pakistanis Intikhab and Mushtaq, not forgetting the Indian Engineer and the Australian McKenzie. Most of our side were rusty by the time the series began but we had the greater talent and won by a four to one margin. This was the series when Ray Illingworth really stamped his authority on the England side as skipper, going on to Australia later that year to regain the Ashes. Ray batted very well against us and he shrewdly made the most of his limited resources against such talented opposition. For most of the series, I batted at number eight, behind men like Sobers, Pollock, Lloyd and Kanhai, but on a few occasions I had to earn my keep with the bat as Illingworth inspired his team to play above themselves.

In the first Test at Lord's, I ruined poor Alan Jones's one and only Test – c Engineer b Procter for 5 and 0 – and we won by an innings, with Sobers making 183. Eddie Barlow also made a hundred, an innings I thought one of the best I've ever seen. Barlow lacked the genius of a Sobers and he'd only just arrived over from South Africa. He was out of practice, felt very rusty, and throughout his innings hardly played a shot I could remember. But he refused to give it away and his knock was one of sheer character and guts. Eddie's attitude throughout that series was, 'I'm the most talented guy in this outfit and don't you forget it', and even if this was untrue, he still gave it all he had. He took a hat-trick in the Headingley game, scored two centuries and topped the bowling averages. A remarkable man, Eddie Barlow; he never saw why he should struggle with either bat or ball.

At Trent Bridge, we contrived to throw away the match by 8 wickets but we won the next, at Edgbaston, by 5 wickets. This was the game which gave me an interesting insight into the mind of an English groundsman. Having been playing over in England since 1968, I still couldn't get over the slowness of the wickets and I longed for a few bouncy tracks to encourage me to bowl even quicker. Before the match at Edgbaston the groundsman told me that he'd worked on the wicket for the past ten days and that it would be a hard, fast one. I licked my lips, especially when we fielded first and I opened the bowling. My first ball bounced twice after passing the batsman on the way through to the wicket-keeper! So much for fond hopes.

In the next game, at Headingley, we nearly caught a cold. We needed just 223 to win, but slumped to 183 for 8. Barry Richards, with an injured back, came out to join me, with just Lance Gibbs to come. Now things were getting a little keyed up out there, not least because the England boys were playing for their places on the trip to Australia, and also because £2,000 was at stake for the winners. John Snow took the new ball, and one delivery flew off Barry's pad to Don Wilson at short leg. They all went up in the air for the catch, but the umpire turned it down. Some of the England boys thought Barry should have walked, but honestly I don't think he touched it. Anyway, we crept home after I decided to chance my arm. Barry came down the wicket and told me to take it easy, but I thought, 'He can hardly move, Gibbs can't bat, I'm getting a move on', so I drove one over mid-off for one 4 and then sliced another over the slips' heads for a second. They all count when there's a match to be won.

The last game at the Oval was especially memorable for the sight of the two best left-handers in the world sharing a stand of 150-odd. Graeme Pollock hadn't enjoyed a particularly successful tour – he was bowled a lot, possibly because he was playing out of season and not moving his feet quickly enough – but in this game he gave the English crowd a glimpse of his greatness. In a magnificent partnership he overshadowed Gary Sobers and made a beautiful century. The match was won by us by 4 wickets after we'd slumped to 92 for 3, chasing 283. Kanhai got a century and we managed it, but the main talking point was the batting of Pollock. To think that was the last time he ever played in a big match in England. He was just twenty-six.

That 1970 series in England was marvellous fun and the cricket was competitive and enjoyable. But I couldn't help wishing I'd worn the Springbok cap in those five Tests; a Rest of the World side is the next best thing, but nothing can compare with playing for your country. We were bursting to play for South Africa at that time and, in our youthful foolishness, we all thought our isolation would last just a few years. But as the years passed, I became more disillusioned and finally philosophical. I watched the World Cup on television in 1975 and wondered how South Africa would have fared against the other countries. The following year I saw Richards, Greenidge and Lloyd hammer the English bowlers all over the place and wished I could have pitted my wits against them or watched Graeme Pollock bat against Roberts, Holding and Co. But there was eventually no point in brooding about lost opportunities. I can't exactly remember when I gave up real hope of playing Test cricket again – perhaps when the World Series Cricket offer came along – but my Test career now seems a long, long time ago.

3

Kerry Packer

Signing for Kerry Packer was the easiest decision I've ever had to make. As far as I was concerned, the issues were clear cut: I had no future in Test cricket, the money was tremendous, the contract didn't conflict with the one I had with Gloucestershire and it offered security for myself and my family. I didn't even consult my solicitor about the small print of the World Series Cricket contract; I signed as soon as I talked it over with my wife.

World Series Cricket must have been one of the best-kept sporting secrets of all time. How it took so long to leak out is beyond me, because so many people were involved. My first inkling came early in 1977 in South Africa, when Graeme Pollock told me, 'Don't sign a new contract for next season over here. Something's going to happen in Australia that'll interest you, and Tony Greig will get in touch with you soon.' I had a good job with Natal and was fairly settled, but this sounded intriguing. Like many cricketers, I felt that the game was ripe for a takeover by some enterprising tycoon. Later in the year the Australian cricketers told me that the cleaners who swept up the Test grounds at close of play were getting more money than the players, so you can see that Lillee and Co. had a legitimate gripe.

When I returned to England in the spring of 1977 Tony Greig rang me and told me to go to the Churchill Hotel in London for an important meeting. On Easter Monday I walked into the hotel to find Eddie Barlow, Barry Richards, Alan Knott, Dennis Amiss, John Snow and Derek Underwood in the same room. Tony Greig stood up and outlined the plan. It sounded great. We would get 25,000 Australian dollars a year plus bonus money for three years. If you were injured and couldn't play, you'd still get the full whack. We discussed the pros and cons fully and the English guys all realised it would probably mean the end of their Test careers. Nobody was pushed into signing a contract, we were all given plenty of time to think it over. Nothing was mentioned about a possible ban from county cricket but the current Test players at that meeting knew that they were putting their Test careers on the block – Tony Greig was the England captain, after all, and an England tour of Pakistan and New Zealand was scheduled at the same time as the Packer matches later that year.

Many have asked me what I would have done about Packer if I'd been a current Test player. I'd like to think I would have done the honourable thing but, to be honest, I think I still would have signed for World Series Cricket. After all, South Africa hadn't played many Tests when we were still in the fold, because the black countries wouldn't walk on to the same field as us so there were often gaps of three years between Test matches involving South Africa. As far as the South Africans were concerned, this was a great chance to get back to top-class competition again; for someone like Graeme Pollock there was no dilemma because he played as an amateur in the Currie Cup and earned his money as manager of a protective clothing firm.

It was obvious we had to keep quiet about the deal. I never mentioned it to Gloucestershire because I didn't see that my career in county cricket clashed with what I did in an English winter. My county colleague, Zaheer Abbas, also signed for Packer and of course we talked about the deal privately. He had no qualms about it; like most of the guys, he thought the money was too good to turn down. When the news broke early in May, I was at a club cocktail party and I got some sour looks from several Gloucestershire officials. Our secretary, Tony Brown, said, 'If you want to join Packer, that's your decision, but you probably won't be able to play for us after this season.' I just didn't know what was going to happen in that respect, so I concentrated all my energies on my first season as Gloucestershire's captain. We won the Benson and Hedges Cup that year as I tried hard to concentrate on my cricket.

I'd never heard of Kerry Packer or Channel 9 television until April 1977. I'd no idea he was such a big noise over in Australia, otherwise I might have been more respectful to him when he told me I was a little overweight at our first meeting – 'You get in the nets, I'll bowl at you and we'll see how fit I am' was my blunt reaction. I think he liked my plain speaking, because we always got on very well. I think he's a great guy and I admire the way he gets things done. He got totally involved with the players and backed us all the way; he knew more about cricket than he was ever given credit for and I respect the fact that he stays loyal to staff who are the same to him. Now I know people will say I've been brainwashed, but I don't care. Anybody who knows me will realise I'm not the type to be taken in easily by someone waving money around. There's much more to Kerry Packer than that.

I got involved with the famous case in the High Court in London because I felt I owed some sort of public demonstration of my respect for Kerry Packer. I was one of the three men nominated to take the Test and County

Cricket Board to court (Snow and Greig were the others), and it all started when Tony Greig rang me at a Bristol restaurant one night and told me to get down to London at once. I got to the Dorchester just after midnight to find Packer's suite crawling with lawyers. The TCCB and the ICC wanted to ban Packer players from Test and first-class cricket and we were trying for an injunction to prevent this. There was no pressure on me to get involved in the court case, but I was happy to do so because it was in the interests of World Series Cricket and, I believed, cricketers generally.

I had no doubt that we would win and I enjoyed the experience. I'd never been to court before and I was nervous. I listened intently to all the legal rigmarole and marvelled at how long it took the lawyers to get to the point of their interrogations. Every day we had lunch with our QC and we weren't allowed to discuss the court proceedings. I spoke in court for about an hour and half and stayed with the case for about ten days before flying home to South Africa. The impression I got from the TCCB's submissions was that any player who has represented his country would end up with a good job when his career ended – but that was surely wrong. As Tony Greig pointed out when questioned, he may have been captain at the time of signing for Packer, but for how long? He had no guarantee of security and vague promises don't pay the bills.

It came out in court that Packer had offered six times as much as ABC Television for exclusive TV rights of Test cricket coverage but the Australian Board turned him down because they'd dealt with ABC for years. That seemed incredible to me and when the news came through in Melbourne that the TCCB had lost the case, I felt no sympathy for them. The game is short of cash in England, yet the counties had sanctioned court-case costs of £200,000 for a hopeless cause.

During that 1977 season there was a definite 'WSC v the Rest' atmosphere in county dressing rooms, but I honestly feel the critics of Packer would have signed if given the chance. A lot of the backbiting stemmed from jealousy, but my philosophy is that the better players get the best. The English Packer players took a lot of flak that season for opting out of the official winter tour but, as far as I was concerned, facing up to Holding, Roberts, Lillee and Co. in Australia would be far tougher than batting on Pakistan wickets against a limited bowling attack.

That first series of Packer matches lasted from November to February in Australia and, although a lot of things were against us, we were all determined to try our damnedest to make it work. There was a fair amount of travelling and personal appearances but not as many as some of the players moaned about. As far as I was concerned, we were getting superb money plus the chance to play high-class international cricket, so there was just no point in complaining about the hard work involved. There was no set routine. We might play a couple of night games, then a one-day match in the country, then back to Melbourne or Sydney for a Super Test over four days. The up-country games were often played in front of about 250 spectators and the anti-Packer brigade had a field day; but often we play in front of 300 people in county cricket and nobody says that's on the skids. The wickets weren't very good in the country games. But it was a good public relations exercise for cricket and we helped spread the word in areas that official touring sides rarely visited.

We had teething problems at the start. A lot of the press were pro-establishment and we were banned from practising on many grounds. I bowled the first ball of World Series Cricket to Rick McCosker at VFL Park in Melbourne and, to be honest, the feeling that day was a hollow one. The crowd was terribly disappointing, considering that about 5,000 had turned up to see the Packer

Aussies practising in the nets a few days earlier. One consolation, though: the wickets at Melbourne and Sydney were superb, with pace and even bounce. They were the work of a fantastic groundsman, John Maley, who produced them in a greenhouse. Our wicket at the Sydney showground was a better one than the Test match wickets at the Sydney cricket ground and all credit to Maley. He did more for World Series Cricket than any player because he gave us good wickets in the big matches.

There's no doubt that many people thought that Packer cricket was simply a circus in that first year. The official Australian team played an exciting home series with the Indians, even if the overall standard wasn't that great; there was a lot of talk about 'fair dinkum' cricket as played by Bobby Simpson and his team, and also some suggestions that we fixed a few of the matches. Well, all I can say is that those critics didn't see many of our matches. The first Super Test between Australia and the West Indies was the biggest bouncer war I'd yet seen and the toughest match most of the players had experienced. In another game during the two years of WSC, Tony Greig really turned the screws on Joel Garner when he batted with a broken finger. Earlier in that game, Andy Roberts had broken Majid Khan's cheekbone, and Greig and I had been made to look like beginners on a wicket with regular but high bounce. As you can imagine, Joel Garner's height made him an almost impossible proposition when he bowled and Greig and I really struggled. But it was a good batting wicket and I remember Bill Lawry saying on TV that the West Indies would win comfortably after we were bowled out for just over 100. Anyway, I happened to mention to Joel before their innings that the ball tends to follow something like a broken finger, and as it happened he had a bad time of it when he came in to bat. The score was 60-odd for 9 and

Tony Greig, remembering his humiliation at the hands of Garner, called for three bouncers in a row. The first one hit him straight on his broken finger and Joel walked off in disgust. That shows there was no quarter given to anyone in our so-called 'circus' games.

In the first year of WSC, I counted fourteen separate head injuries to batsmen; something like that was bound to happen with the world's fastest bowlers all trying to outdo each other. In a three- or five-day game, you can duck and weave out of the way of these guys, but in a limited-over match, you had to try to score quick runs. A lot of people laughed at Dennis Amiss when he wore the helmet, but within a few days we were all queueing up to use it. The worst injury was to David Hookes when Andy Roberts broke his jaw. If he'd been wearing a helmet he would have been safe. With all the speed stuff flying around your ears, you had to adjust your batting style: you had to play a lot more off the back foot and you hardly ever saw a cover drive, one of my favourite shots. A lot of people criticised WSC for concentrating on the physical side of bowling to the detriment of the spinners. Well, there were people like Underwood, Padmore, Bright and Mallett in the shake-up, but it's true that speed dominated things. I was often fifth-choice bowler in my side, but Lillee, Thomson, Roberts, Holding, Snow, Procter and Co. had all made their names in Test cricket and I feel sure that if WSC had happened at another stage of cricket history the dominant, match-winning bowlers of that time would have played the major role. After all, the great Indian spinners, Bedi and Chandra were both lined up for the third abortive season of WSC.

There was a good relationship between the sides, but when we got on the field, it was the toughest cricket I've known. I don't think the prize money had anything to do with that, I think we all relished the competition and the high quality of the cricket. And there was plenty of aggro between certain players – particularly Ian Chappell and Tony Greig. These two never really got on and things came to a head in the Grand Final of the Super Tests; we were playing for prize money of 80,000 Australian dollars and Greigy, as usual, had fanned the flames with a newspaper article a couple of days beforehand, in which he said he was the man for the big occasion and he was going to put an end to his poor form. This ignored the fact that Greig was only in the World side because we had to release some of the Pakistanis for a Test match but things like that would never shake his self-confidence. Anyway, the Aussies were a bit choked because they hadn't won too many games and they weren't too happy with Greigy's remarks. Ian Chappell got the article photostatted and the Aussies got gee'd up by reading it on the way to the ground. When Greig came out to bat, Lillee fired four bouncers in a row at him and then Marsh caught him behind for nought. There were no complaints from Greig but the Aussies were beside themselves with joy. We managed to win the match by five wickets, but it was really close and in the second innings, Imran Khan came in ahead of Greig. That annoyed the Aussies, because they were looking forward to having another go at the man they loved to hate. We needed just two runs to win when Ian Chappell grabbed the ball off Pascoe, bowled a very high wide and ran off the field as it trickled down to the boundary. He was choked off at losing the game.

Anyway, Fred Trueman presented the cup and the cheque after the Aussies took a quarter of an hour to come out of their dressing-room. They went past us, shaking hands, and Ian Chappell came to my group. He said, 'Well played' to me and the same to Garth Le Roux and then he automatically put out his hand to the next guy – until he realised that was Greig. He dropped his hand and snarled, 'Nice contribution from you, you ...' and walked off to the next player. Greigy just laughed and started taunting Chappell during the medals ceremony. Afterwards, Chappell walked into our dressing-room and when Greigy saw him he told him: ' . . . . off out of here.' I don't think Greig was anywhere near as bad as Chappell when it came to aggro on the field, but they sure sparked each other off. Funny really, because I know that deep down they respect each other for the stance they've taken against the cricket establishment. I got on well with Chappell, but he wasn't too happy with me that night, either. By the end of the evening, I was well pleased with a large intake of champagne and also with the fact that most of the South Africans (myself, Richards, Le Roux and Rice) had done well in the Grand Final. I told Chappell that the game would have been over a day earlier if there'd been more South Africans in the side! That went down really well.

Another incident I recall which proves that there was absolutely no rigging of matches: the time when Andy Roberts and Dennis Lillee fell out. In the final of the one-day competition, things had got very tight and Lillee took a magnificent diving catch on the boundary to get rid of Roberts. According to the TV playback, he'd just touched the boundary rope as he caught it, but he couldn't have known this. But the West Indian players saw it, told Roberts he'd been unfairly dismissed, and later that night there was some aggro between the two fast bowlers in the hotel.

WSC was hard off the field as well, especially after night cricket. The Super Tests were played over four days and if we played at VFL Park, we would have to travel twenty miles out of Melbourne to be at the ground for midday. We'd start at 1.30 in the afternoon, play till 10.30, get back to the hotel at midnight, take an hour or so to unwind after the hectic day's play and then be up again at 9 o'clock next morning. A lot of the players complained about the long hours, but I think they exaggerated. Cricketers must be the hardest sportsmen to please – they moan about having to get to certain places on time, about the food and having to do a few promotional pieces for their employer. As far as I was concerned, I was lucky to be there. We got a fair amount of time to ourselves, our families were with us, the money was tremendous and we were playing with and against most of the top performers in our chosen profession. Of course there was too much one-day cricket, but that was the kind of stuff the public wanted to see. I can see how frustrating it must have been for some of the WSC players as they tried to break through from the second XI (in the country circuit) to the big stuff in the Super Tests. The batsmen in particular had to battle in limited-over cricket, so it was difficult to get any consistency going, because they always had to keep an eye on the clock and chance their arm. Psychologically a batsman needs a few long innings to get him into good nick and the crowded schedule didn't give much chance of that. But surely top-class sport is all about taking your chances and playing to the best of your abilities? If I'd been consigned to the second eleven stuff, I wouldn't have complained, because in the end the remedy would have been in my hands – on the field.

Many players simply fell by the wayside in the two years of WSC; people like Mushtaq, Amiss and Woolmer didn't do themselves justice while men like Laird, Pascoe, Rice and Le Roux really blossomed. The most spectacular fall from grace was that of Tony Greig. His performances for Sussex were inconsistent, but he could usually raise his game for the big occasion and his Test record is very good indeed. But he hardly bowled in WSC and the way he batted meant he always seemed likely to go through a bad patch, because he just didn't battle for runs. Early in the first season, he wafted one to cover when we were in a dodgy situation and I said, 'How the hell can he play a shot like that at this stage of the game?' only to be told by the English lads that he often played like that in a Test match. Also Greigy was never a fitness fanatic and he relied a lot on match practice to get himself fit. Finally he dropped himself from the World Side and as a co-selector I admired his honesty, but he really only had himself to blame: as captain, he was never with the World Side in the nets on the eve of a Super Test – he was always off doing a commercial or a TV interview.

I'm sure he regrets getting distracted by the commercial side of the game so soon, because he was a great trier on the field, who surpassed his natural abilities by dint of effort, character and temperament. Cricket almost seemed secondary to Greig, he had so much going for him commercially in Australia. They loved him in the media world but I wish he'd been able to do more on the field as the World captain. Still, I'll always respect him for helping to get WSC started. It's easy to criticise him for being disloyal to England but they forget – he was the *last* England captain, not the *next* and one or two more games could have finished him in Test cricket.

Throughout the two years of WSC, we were always conscious of a gulf between ourselves and Establishment cricket. All sorts of snide remarks were made about coloured clothing, the artificiality of the games, the dominance of fast bowlers, the apparent lack of national identity and the poor crowds. Well, the crowds for the two Test series weren't that great either. The Australian public don't like to see their side losing, and when Mike Brearley's team thrashed them 5–1, the attendance figures were very poor. And in that second season, our crowd figures were much better. There seemed a surfeit of cricket in Australia in the 1978/79 season, but the Establishment showed no sign of willingness to compromise. That was made clear to us when we bumped into the

England team at Sydney airport. Only Randall and Boycott said 'hello' to my knowledge, and they were very offhand, considering many of us play against each other and share a few drinks every season in England. Presumably they were under instructions from their management, but it all seemed rather unnecessary.

By March 1979 every one involved with WSC was really looking forward to the third season. We'd started off at rock bottom, but we'd worked hard, night cricket had caught the public's imagination and there seemed every reason for optimism. Then it ended as suddenly as it had begun. In May 1979 I had a phone call from one of the officials, Austin Robertson, to tell me that there'd be an announcement the next day and meanwhile to say nothing to the media about the disbandment of WSC. I had no inkling of this and I was dumbfounded – I'd even left my kit in Australia for the third season. And, more important, I'd shaken hands on a deal with Lynton Taylor, one of Channel 9's top administrators, that I thought had secured me an even brighter financial security. I told Lynton Taylor towards the end of the second season that I would be delighted to sign on for another three years after my present three-year contract had elapsed. We even got down to discussing air fares for my wife and children, and Clive Rice remembers me coming out of the meeting, saying, 'I've got another contract, Lynton and I have shaken hands on it.' But after WSC was disbanded, Lynton denied it.

I was very upset, because I felt that a verbal contract at that stage was sufficient. I can understand Lynton may have suffered from a lapse of memory, because he was dealing with the needs of fifty other players, and at the same time WSC was good enough to pay me for the third year of my original contract, even though there was no longer any cricket. But I was sad at the way it was

Barry Richards and myself a few years back (inset) – and then as county cricketers in England (main photo: Patrick Eagar).

Cricket wasn't the only sport to hold my attention at Highbury
Junior School.

My first job after leaving school: selling clothes in Pietarmaritzburg (photo: *Natal Witness*).

Test cricket in 1967 – and I'm about to catch Australia's Bill Lawry at Johannesburg. Unfortunately, it was a no-ball!

Receiving the County Cricketers' Player of the Year Award from
Gary Sobers in 1969 (photo: Ken Kelly).
Ali Bacher, my former Springbok captain, presents me with
Rhodesia's Sportsman of the Year Award (photo: Stuart Darke/
Photomedia Ltd).

GLOUCESTERSHIRE v HAMPSHIRE
at Gloucester on Tuesday 20th June 1972
County Championship.

M.J. PROCTER ct Richards b Holder. 100.

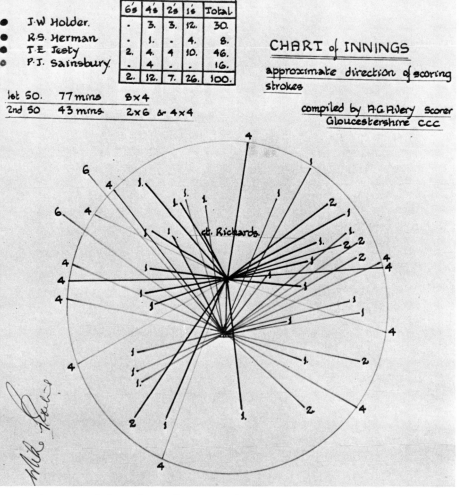

- J·W Holder.
- R·S· Herman
- T·E· Jesty
- P·J· Sainsbury

	6's	4's	2's	1's	Total
	.	3.	3.	12.	30.
	.	1.	.	4.	8.
	2.	4.	4	10.	46.
	.	4	.	.	16.
	2.	12.	7.	26.	100.

CHART of INNINGS

approximate direction of scoring strokes

compiled by A·G· Avery Scorer
Gloucestershire CCC

1st 50.   77 mins   8×4
2nd 50   43 mins   2×6 & 4×4

ct. Richards.

An unusual view of one of my centuries, courtesy of Bert Avery, Gloucestershire's scorer. I recall enjoying Trevor Jesty's bowling that day – but I had no idea where the shots went! (photo: Ken Kelly).

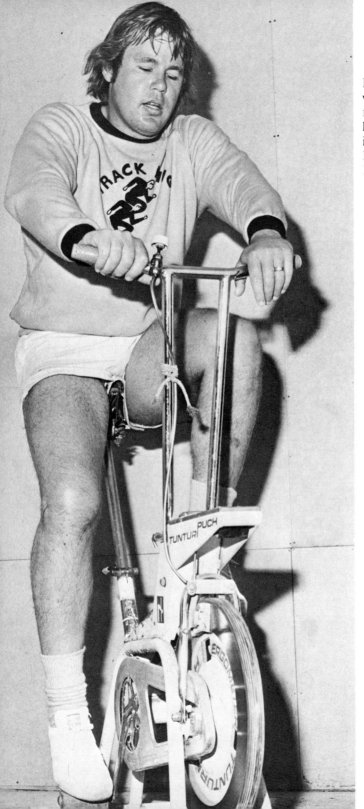

Fighting my way back to fitness after my knee operation in 1975 (photo: Bristol United Press).

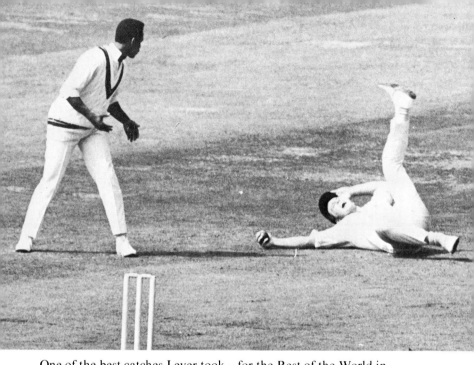

One of the best catches I ever took – for the Rest of the World in
1970 at Headingley. Alan Knott had tried to push Eddie Barlow
past square leg, but he misjudged the line and it squirted to me
at slip (photo: Sport & General).

Enjoying a drink with Eddie Barlow and Edward Abane, one of
the best non-white cricketers South Africa has known.

A great moment in my career as captain – holding the Benson
and Hedges Cup for Gloucestershire in 1977 (photo: Ken Kelly).

disbanded so suddenly and to this day, I don't know why Kerry Packer packed it in.

So the great adventure was over. There had been mistakes – the tour of New Zealand was a disaster, with poor wickets, crowds and weather. Perhaps we saturated the public with too much cricket, at the same time as the official brand of Tests was being played. Perhaps some players were over the hill when they were signed up. It was a shame that the coloured players were not allowed by their Boards of Control to play with or against my fellow-South Africans, Denys Hobson and Graeme Pollock, just because they hadn't played against coloured men in English county cricket. Anybody who knows Hobson and Pollock will tell you that they've done as much as any white South African to help non-whites achieve sporting equality.

But the gains were greater. The quality of play was higher than the Rest of the World series in England in 1970, which many of the Establishment raved about. Night cricket was a magnificent experience and the white ball and coloured clothing eventually worked. Establishment cricket has been happy to embrace those innovations. And television benefited: the standard of camera work was tremendously high, and the various graphics brought the game home to the layman. If some of the commentators weren't the best, nevertheless there were enough of them to go around. Even the BBC has seen fit to use some of the techniques of Channel 9's cricket coverage.

Above all, it was not only the cricketers who signed for him whose financial lot Packer helped to improve. He acted as a catalyst for the minimum wage structure in English county cricket, something the authorities had been dragging their heels over for many years. Tony Greig was derided when he said the average county cricketer would benefit from WSC, but they have. More people are interested in cricket because of Packer's influence and it's a strange coincidence that Test fees suddenly went up from £250 to £1,000 in the summer of 1977, when English players were defecting to WSC. It might have taken several years to get the fees up to that level, but Packer helped to force the TCCB's hand. He made cricket a more commercial sport. I don't go along with Barry Richards's theory that we should get as much as tennis stars or top golfers, because we just don't reach the same sort of audience, and cricket is also a team game, but the fact remains that Packer helped us throw away the begging bowl.

Packer also helped the cricketer who is a family man. Our wives were with us on the tour and there were nurseries for our children, so that we could leave them in good hands whenever we fancied some time on our own. A strong family tie was the main reason why Greg Chappell packed up Test cricket before WSC started, and all those who've been grateful for his subsequent change of heart can thank Packer for that. He'd just had enough of overseas tours and those two seasons helped him rediscover the happiness of a close family.

There was a lot of humbug written and talked about the Packer affair. Some of the worst was over the alleged disloyalty of the England players who opted out of Test cricket. But for as long as I can remember, the top English players have decided when they want to tour. What about Ted Dexter, who initially opted out of the trip to South Africa in 1964 because he was standing for Parliament in the general election? Or Chris Old, who stayed at home to organise his benefit and recharge his batteries instead of making himself available for Australia? And how many English players have dipped out of a tour to India or Pakistan because they didn't fancy the food or the climate? Then there's Geoff Boycott – he opts out of Test cricket for three years because he doesn't approve of the captains, turns up at the Centenary Test in 1977 because he was playing grade cricket in Australia, then decides to make himself available again later in 1977 when it suits him. He's then rewarded with the vice-captaincy of his country on the winter tour of Pakistan and New Zealand. Of course he turned down Packer and the Establishment loved him for that – but Boycott didn't need the money, being one of the few cricketers to make a tidy living before Packer. And I also suspect he realised the style of cricket wouldn't suit his particular brand of batting.

In years to come, when Kerry Packer is a distant memory, his critics may be a little kinder in their judgement of him and what he did for cricket. He certainly helped Michael John Procter become a better player.

4

Cricket in England

Having played professional cricket in South Africa, Australia and Rhodesia, I suppose my credentials for examining the state of English cricket are quite good. At least I've seen how it's played and administered in other countries – unlike many who pontificate at some length about English cricket's pros and cons.

When I first came over to England as a professional in 1968 the game was dying on its feet. Apart from the County Championship, the Gillette Cup was the only other competition and there was very little sponsorship. Looking back on it all now, 1968 seems a bygone age – we enjoyed Sundays off, when we could play golf, or turn out in a charity match, or even just lounge around reading the papers or watching TV. That air of relaxation (and of course, the bitter cold) are my principal memories of that year, as I found my feet in county cricket.

Today's brand of English cricket is action-packed in comparison. There are now four competitions, all generously sponsored. There's the Schweppes County Championship, the National Westminster Cup (formerly the Gillette), the John Player League and the Benson and Hedges Cup. The last three are limited-overs competitions, while the County Championship was limited to 100

overs on the first innings until 1981. I think it's right to
utilise all the days you can in an English summer, so there
are no complaints from me about playing on Sundays; the
travelling becomes a drag but we are, after all, professional cricketers and we're far better treated than at the start
of my county career.

It's now much harder work to play county cricket year
in, year out, but the rewards are better. Most capped
players get a free car thrown in, the status of a county
cricketer has improved and even the food is better. When
I first came to Bristol, we had to go down the road for a
pint of milk and a pie during pre-season training, but now
we get all sorts of hot dinners and hardly ever a salad.
Good grub is a subject that's very important to English
cricketers, I find. If you mention where the next game is,
you can bet someone will say something like, 'Oh good/
damn, the snap's bloody good/horrible there!' The facilities at Bristol now are fantastic: squash courts, saunas,
excellent training facilities.

In the old days lunch on match day would be something
like a piece of meat with a quarter tomato and lettuce and
one boiled potato, but now it's a choice of hot meals. All
this may sound pretty insignificant, but not if you have to
go out and field on a freezing cold day against Clive
Lloyd. Apart from that, the improved facilities in county
cricket have made the players realise they're not whiling
away their days in a dying sport.

Now that World Series Cricket is no more, I think the
county game is the most consistently competitive brand of
cricket in the world, apart from Tests. In South Africa,
there's a lot of tension and edge over the Currie Cup
matches, but there aren't very many of them. In England,
you've got the chance to develop your skills and pit them
against other players for almost every day in a four month
period. The fact that there are four competitions also

helps the English pro to be a more philosophical character than his overseas counterpart. In county cricket you can try your damnedest, but even if you lose there's always tomorrow and another game. Overseas, you get wound up to a pitch because there are so few chances to play competitively at a high level. This diversity in the English game gives it a terrific amateur spirit in the way it's played professionally. It's hard, of course, but you meet some great blokes around the counties and there's no shortage of laughs to be had. Some sides are particularly welcome at Bristol, because you know they'll play it the right way on and off the field.

The travelling is a big drag, especially on a Saturday night when you've got to travel to a hotel after playing that day and get ready for a Sunday League match. Then, after the Sunday game is over, you get in the car and drive back to the first hotel to continue the three-day Championship match. It was worse in my first few years, when there weren't so many motorways, but it's still a pain in the neck now. In an English season, I'll travel about 10,000 miles, involving trips like Taunton to Manchester on the Saturday night, then back to Taunton the night after (about 450 miles in all). I'm amazed that county cricketers aren't involved in more car accidents because it's very tiring on the motorway when you've been playing all day. You notice how attitudes change halfway through the season; at the start everyone's rushing around, full of zest and requests for extra training, but by mid-season, you're gone and the travelling's the main reason.

Just one example of the travelling involved in English cricket; at the end of one county match at Birmingham, I drove up to Scarborough on the Friday to play in a double wicket competition. The following evening I motored back down to stay in Birmingham, en route for a charity match at Tavistock in Devon on the Sunday. On the Tuesday I drove home to Bristol – a round trip of 1,400 miles since Friday night, a total of twenty-two hours driving!

Travelling up and down the county circuit in England leads to a very schizophrenic life-style. Most of our players go to bed at about ten o'clock when they're at home, whereas on away trips we often have a few beers and late nights. It can get lonely and frustrating in hotel after hotel, and the best thing to do is make the best of it. So our players stick together in the evenings and a few drinks don't do team spirit any harm at all.

In my time in England, the fielding has improved tremendously. When I first started, every side had a few 'camels' in the field, who were usually opening bowlers or specialist batsmen, but now the standard is very high. Undoubtedly the extra fitness demands caused by the growth of one-day cricket hastened the retirement of several fine cricketers, but the improved fielding has definite spectator appeal. The crowds love to see someone diving around all over the place and this emphasis on fitness and anticipation of scoring shots has spread to all levels of the game in England. It is particularly gratifying to a bowler when he bowls a bad ball and a superb piece of fielding gets him off the hook.

So better fielding is one major gain from limited-overs cricket. So is the extra cash and public appeal, something one can easily judge by looking at the number of children who always clamour for autographs at matches. In my experience autograph hunting is most popular in England at the moment and that's all to the good of the game. It means that the children are coming in to the games, buying the magazines or watching matches on television. The one-day brand of cricket must take some credit for popularising it.

Unfortunately, this kind of cricket is getting very stereotyped. The John Player League shows up the worst kind of defensiveness at the moment. Its forty-overs structure means that the weaker bowling sides have a reasonable chance of papering over their frailties. So they ring the boundary with eight or nine fielders, ask the bowler to bowl line-and-length and invite the batsman to commit suicide or just pick off ones and twos. There's no variety in that – it's artificial and boring. I think they should introduce a law whereby a certain amount of fielders must be within twenty-five yards of the bat. This way the lesser batsman would struggle while the class player would think; 'Five men out, four men in to save one – let's see where I can get some boundaries.' At the moment, it doesn't matter whether you're Graeme Pollock or Joe Bloggs, defensive field placing is producing boredom.

The one-day game is basically about containment, with little else but line-and-length bowling and reliance on good fielding. The three-day Championship game remains the true test and the competition we all really want to win. But the hundred-overs limitation on first innings made it just an extension of the other three competitions, which range from forty to sixty overs. Until the overs limit was scrapped, a Championship game on a flat wicket against a good batting side meant that (short of a fine piece of bowling by somebody) we would be back to a one-day mentality after about seventy-five overs. I'd go on the defensive, try to minimise their total and not worry too much about bowling them out. It became a batsman's game, where they could pick off plenty of ones and twos and then the captains had to jockey over declarations on the final morning to try to force a positive result. More artificiality!

No wonder England haven't discovered many men who can bowl sides out on good wickets in recent years. They don't get much chance to develop their bowling skills, because they've been encouraged by the structure of three-

day cricket simply to keep batsmen quiet. The decline in
spinners stems from the same situation: they become an
expensive commodity if they like to buy their wickets, so
they learn to bowl flat and contain. If they're lucky
enough to get into the England side, they come up against
Richards or Gavaskar or Chappell on a flat wicket and
two days bowling stretching ahead – and they struggle.

England won't become a world-class side again until
they alter the shape of the Championship. My own
solution is for sixteen four-day games with covered
wickets, so that the bowlers will really have to work for
their wickets by intelligence and discipline, rather than
just expecting an average seamer to pitch it on the same
spot from the eightieth over onwards. Four-day cricket
would appeal to sponsors because it gives them an extra
day's advertising round the ground, the public would like
to return to the days when batsmen scored triple
hundreds, it would be a better grounding for young
players who may go on to Test cricket and it would then
be far removed from the financially necessary one-day
stuff. And it would end that crude slogging and scamper-
ing for bonus points.

A Test batsman (unless he's a genius like Viv Richards)
doesn't make hundreds in two hours, he has to graft
against good bowling and fielding. Great English players
like May, Cowdrey, Dexter and Graveney learned their
trade away from the hurly-burly of limited-overs regula-
tions; they acquired mental discipline, variety of stroke
play and big match temperament in games that relied on
the goodwill of the captains to make them into good
cricket matches, as well as allowing opportunities for
personal success. Presumably the introduction of the
hundred-overs limit into county cricket was an indictment
of the defensive attitudes of the captains. Well, speaking
as Gloucestershire's captain, I'd be happy to play the
four-day stuff, secure in the knowledge that I'd

have more chance of getting a positive result than I have at the moment. In recent years there's been very little elbow-room in championship matches unless the wicket plays up, the weather intervenes, or someone bowls very well.

Some of the blame for this state of affairs lies at the door of groundsmen. The wickets in England are getting slower and slower every year. All players would like even bounce and extra pace on wickets, but that just doesn't seem possible. This discourages the spin bowler further, because the ball doesn't turn quickly enough; it does nothing for a genuinely fast bowler, because the ball won't fizz off the wicket. That's why England has had so few genuinely quick bowlers in my time over here: Bob Willis and, towards the end of the seventies, Graham Dilley have been the only ones. Fast bowling is hard, physical work and English wickets don't exactly encourage them. Bob Willis has been the quickest English fast bowler for a very long time now and that's not only in praise of a great-hearted trier, but also an indictment of the kind of slow wickets that are prepared in England. I can only think of a handful of good, fast wickets in my time over here that have helped the strokemaker, the quick bowler and the spinner: Hove, Worcester, Leeds and Chesterfield and, on occasions, Bristol.

Now first-class cricketers don't know all that much about the preparation of wickets and I'm no exception. But my theory is that wickets just get too old; the more they are watered and rolled, the slower they get. I think they should be dug up regularly and a new one laid – that's what happened at Bristol when I first came over. I used to sweat and strain to get the ball above stump height but when the groundsman dug up one end of the square, the ball came off as quickly as anywhere in England for a couple of years. But now it varies dramatically in speed and bounce.

The slow English wickets have a lot to do with the late maturing of many English batsmen. With the ball moving about off the seam so much, you need a defensive technique to combat it; that's why most overseas players take a couple of seasons to get used to English conditions, where the ball keeps low and takes time to come on to the bat. My old Gloucestershire colleague Arthur Milton always maintained that it takes ten years to learn to play the game properly in England and he may well be right. Arthur, who opened the batting for England, says overseas players mature so much faster because they learn their trade on firmer wickets, while the English boy has to learn to survive before he can play shots. That may be so, but I tend to think confidence to play your shots is just as important. That's something young English batsmen like Gower and Botham possess, and they were brought up on slow wickets as well. I wonder if the English batsman gets his mind fixed on blaming a slow wicket for his lack of strokeplay?

There are other reasons, besides slow wickets, that are trotted out for the lack of top-class English cricketers. The main one is the presence of so many overseas players in the County Championship. A glance at the national averages for any recent season proves the point that overseas players dominate both bowling and batting sections, but let's be honest – on average only about two men per team are *not* qualified to play for England. The reason why the overseas cricketers dominate the county scene is because so many of them are high-class performers. The county officials know that, so do the sponsors. Would the one-day competitions have been so successful in the last decade without people like Lloyd, Richards, and Kanhai? Without them I don't think the County Championship would have survived in its present form.

Alec Bedser, the chairman of England's selectors, is

always trotting out overseas players as a major reason for England's poor Test performances. I remember when he cited Lancashire's Frank Hayes as an example of a talented English player who had been denied his true chance to flower because Clive Lloyd was batting above him. I would have thought it was easier for Hayes to follow Lloyd, because if he bats with Clive, there's no pressure on Hayes to get quick runs. Lloyd is such a good, fast-scoring batsman that his partner just needs to chug along quietly, playing himself in and giving Lloyd as much of the strike as possible, then taking over when he gets out. Conversely, walking in to bat after the bowlers have been smashed around by Lloyd is surely an enjoyable prospect. The bowlers could well be demoralised after being thrashed around the park, and a talented player like Hayes would find them fairly undemanding.

I think Alec Bedser knew there just weren't enough good young English players around when he criticised Lancashire over Frank Hayes. In any event, he can't tell me that the presence of two or three overseas players in a team constitutes a major threat to a young Englishman's Test career. An overseas player can only bat or bowl at one end and other cricketers *are* allowed to join in, you know. It's true that the limited-overs nature of English cricket means that the first batting places are the most important and that overseas players like Glenn Turner, Peter Kirsten, John Wright, Zaheer Abbas and Alvin Kallicharran occupy some of these key positions – but not all of them. And the fact that fast bowlers like Daniel, Clarke, Roberts, Rice, Hadlee and others have dominated county cricket over the years is a condemnation of the lack of English fast bowlers and proof that overseas wickets help a quickie learn how to bowl at speed.

But let's put things in perspective. It's true that in the late sixties several counties engaged overseas stars who didn't do themselves justice and perhaps jaundiced a few opinions about overseas players. But the majority of overseas players who've been here for some time are genuinely attached to their counties and have a true regard for the supporters and club officials. The numbers are being limited gradually and the vast majority of county sides contain men eligible to play for England – but not good enough. Professional cricket in England is more interested in quick success now than at any other stage in my career and overseas players will continue to play a decisive role in those victories, because they are match-winners as well as crowd-pleasers. Ask Yorkshire: they will only play Yorkshire-born men in their team, yet they haven't won a trophy since 1969, and they've gone through three captains in as many years.

One thing I will criticise a tiny percentage of overseas players for: taking a benefit and then refusing to come back again. A cricketer relies heavily on public support when he organises his benefit and it's kicking all those kind people in the teeth simply to say, 'Thanks a lot, I'll see you all sometime.' I think cricketers should stay on for at least two years if possible after a benefit year. I took mine in 1976 and I wouldn't dream of walking out on those loyal supporters after that. They gave up a lot of precious time to work for my financial security and I'll always be grateful. But it angers me when some critics of overseas players think we're all tarred with the same mercenary brush – people make sweeping generalisations based on rare occurrences.

Despite the presence of so many world-class players, I don't think the standard of ability is all that good in English county cricket. I've never seen an outstanding young English player at the age of eighteen who I knew would make it to the top. I've never even seen one I wouldn't hesitate to put straight into the Gloucestershire First Eleven. This is in complete contrast to the situation in South Africa, where Graeme Pollock scored a double century for Eastern Province at the age of sixteen, Hylton Ackerman played in the Currie Cup at sixteen and Peter Kirsten at the age of seventeen looked a class player when I first saw him. He was playing for Western Province against my Rhodesian side and we crowded him as soon as he came in to bat. He had class written all over him and didn't bother the slightest about the close fielders.

The climate, of course, has got a lot to do with the maturity of young South African cricketers; a great deal of emphasis is placed on sport in the Republic and the hard, bouncy wickets are ideal for batting and bowling. But it goes deeper than just the difference in climate. No other country I know puts as much into sport at school level; promising South African cricketers are caught when young and their skills are fostered by good coaches and superb facilities. When Barry Richards, Hylton Ackerman and myself toured England with the South African Schools side in 1963, we were amazed at how little was done for cricket at school level. And it's got worse; many schools in England no longer play cricket at all and even if they do, the extra emphasis on academic prowess means the cricket term is a hurried, unsatisfactory few weeks.

Compare the Nuffield Schools Week in South Africa, where the best schoolboy cricketers in the Republic pit their skills against each other. The following players passed through the Nuffield entrance exam to a higher level: McGlew, Waite, Bland, Barlow, Richards, Irvine, Lance and myself. And many, many more. Without this policy of fostering cricket at school level, South Africa would not have produced so many fine players in the past couple of decades. Such a system would never work in England. The standards of discipline are completely different; children have a much easier life in England, whereas there's much more discipline in South African schools. I sent my son Gregg to Clifton College, one of the best schools in the Bristol area, and I was amazed to hear that some of the boys call masters by their christian name! At the age of nine! That's not right and it helped make up my mind about sending him home to South Africa to be educated full-time over there.

I'm sure I sound very old-fashioned about this, but I believe discipline is very important at school. Cricket is a very disciplined game and young kids have to learn to buckle down to learning all about it. Perhaps that's why soccer is more popular in English schools; it doesn't take so long to play, you don't have to practise so much, and you can roam around on the field in an undisciplined fashion.

But English professional cricket has many advantages over its counterpart in South Africa. The standard of umpiring is one of the main differences. In England, it's simply the best in the world. Most of the county umpires are former pros, and they know most of the players who will try it on, who is honest, etc. And they're umpiring every day, whereas abroad you can get a bloke standing in a first-class match who hasn't umpired for a couple of weeks. The players respect English umpires because they are fair, they know the game and they won't buckle to pressure from habitual appealers. In South Africa, word gets round that certain umpires in some provinces are dodgy, so you find yourself appealing twice as much on the basis that the more you appeal the more you'll get from him. That attitude stems from a lack of respect and you'd never get that in England. In Australia some umpires won't give lbw decisions when the batsman is on the front foot, or even half-forward, even though the ball is one of full length – but the English umpires let you know where you stand and they're consistent.

Basically umpiring at first-class level is all about making as few mistakes as possible, because you assume the umpire knows the laws. Unfortunately, many umpires in South Africa have buckled under pressure in recent years as the games get more and more competitive, and appealing increases. Lee Irvine came up with an interesting suggestion to try to improve the umpiring standards; he suggested that the umpires should stand in the nets during practice sessions, to get used to making decisions. Lee thought it would sharpen up their skills, and that the players would get to know the umpires better. It never came to fruition but I thought it well worth trying.

In South Africa 'walking' is much more of a problem than in England. This is a personal decision about which I would never dictate to anybody in my side, but I maintain the batsman should be consistent in his attitudes. Either he walks when knows he's touched the ball or he always stays put; to vary the course of action puts extra pressure on the umpire. A few years back, I got together with Barry Richards and Graeme Pollock and we agreed that in our Currie Cup games against each other, we would instruct our players to walk if they knew they were out. As a result we had two very good, sporting games of cricket, all the tension disappeared and the umpires enjoyed it as well. Unfortunately, you can't legislate for a player who disobeys an instruction and refuses to walk when he knows he's out. It would be interesting to see if that would work again.

Although walking is on the decrease in English county cricket, it's still a more sporting game than in other countries. And a lot of the credit for that goes to the strong umpiring and the basic good sense of the players. After all, if everyone knows you've cheated, the opposition fast bowler will soon catch up on you next time you play each other. And in England, you see a lot of the other county sides in a season.

5

Cricket in South Africa

For a long time after we were banned from Test cricket
the game went through the doldrums in South Africa.
There was a general feeling of depression, that we'd
reached the end of the road and that rugby would
consolidate its hold on the sporting affection of the
Republic.

The schools suffered; when we were at the top of the
tree after beating England and Australia, I'm sure that
many young South Africans chose cricketers as their
sporting idols, but it was difficult to gauge the extent of
our abilities in the seventies. Test cricket was the yardstick
for the youngsters, and every time Graeme Pollock scored
a Test hundred, you could bet his example would inspire a
few more children to take an interest in cricket. When I
was a sport-crazy lad at school, I used to fret whenever
rain stopped play; we'd play imaginary 'tests' in the
dormitory and I'd while away the hours picking my World
Eleven and selecting a South African side to play Mars or
the touring party for England. I even filled in a scorebook
of the Springbok tour to England, and compiled the
averages. Not surprisingly South Africa won every game!
To me, the summit of my ambition was to play for South
Africa. I've often wondered since whether my zeal for

cricket would have been so great if I'd not been able to watch giants like McGlew, McLean, Adcock and Waite in home Tests. Isolation might have hit me as hard as it has done the South African kids of the seventies. There was a period when interest in the game at schools was lower than at any stage in my memory.

Things are on the up and up now in South Africa; because of the English county championship, kids have their South African heroes again. It's not the same as Test cricket, I agree, but the coverage of county cricket is so good in South African papers that the youngsters know the standard of competition involved. Some of the best cricketers in the world play in the English county championship and if the South Africans do well in it, that's good for our country's pride. So when people like myself, Allan Lamb and Clive Rice come home after the English season, we can tell how much interest there is in our achievements – and it gets through to the youngsters.

The standard of cricket in the Currie Cup is now the highest it's been for ten years. There was a bad period when a few of us went off to play World Series Cricket. Interest was low, because the sides weren't truly representative in the competition for the Currie Cup. But now, with the disbandment of WSC, all the players are back and there's a lot of tension and high quality cricket. And interest among the public is very high again – one recent Datsun Shield semi-final involving my team (Natal) against Transvaal was played in front of a jam-packed stadium. The average crowds for the Currie Cup games (the equivalent of the English county championship) are about 5,000 a day, which compares very favourably with England. Over the Christmas period, when Western Province play Transvaal, you'll get about 10,000 spectators a day, and there's a great atmosphere, to which the players respond. Normally Currie Cup games start on Friday and last till Monday, missing out Sunday, but in Durban we play straight through and finish on Sunday.

Because there's only one Currie Cup match every three weeks, interest is normally very high when the game comes round. The weather makes a big difference, because you know there's an outstanding chance of uninterrupted play, so there's always a big press build-up before the match. By the time we take the field, we're fresh and raring to go, compared to some days in England, where it's a bit of a slog having to fire yourself for another game.

Club cricket works the same way as in Australia. All the ones who play first-class cricket for their provinces have to play in club cricket and then they're selected for Currie Cup matches from their performances in the club games. So the standard is very high in club cricket in South Africa; everyone's trying their damnedest to get into the Currie Cup games, because that's the only thing that a South African cricketer can aim for at the moment. Everyone talks optimistically about getting back into the international fold, but even if that happens, I hope we don't get too optimistic about our chances of success. In the long run, I believe South Africa would prosper because of the great natural talent of our cricketers, but the Test game is hard and unrelenting now. I had a taste of the standard in World Series Cricket, and you need a strong mental attitude to succeed. You also need to adapt to wickets abroad, and some South African players would struggle initially on soft English wickets. We would be all right on Australian wickets, but it would be a different story in New Zealand. Everybody tells me what a dominant force we would have been in world cricket during the seventies, but perhaps that's a rather optimistic view: success comes in cycles and for a five-year period, ending in 1970, South Africa prospered.

Perhaps we were due for a reversal of fortune. Just a

few injuries to key players would have upset our balance, and don't forget, we never had a top-class spinner in the side, and that would have hampered us in England. I prefer to dwell on the lack of opportunities to test ourselves against other countries, rather than might-have-beens about our superiority. That 1970 Springbok team was a great one, but I know enough about the resilience of Australians to appreciate that they would have been all out to revenge that 4 – 0 thrashing if our tour had gone ahead in 1971/2.

Despite the high quality of playing ability, the game is still essentially amateur in South Africa. Most first-class cricketers over there have regular jobs and they get time off to play in the Currie Cup (it's convenient that these games are played at weekends). It worries me that South Africans have so little incentive to stay in the game, apart from the pleasure of pitting their skills against each other. There's very little money to be made out of first-class cricket in South Africa unless you're playing for the Currie Cup champions, who get prize money from South African Breweries, who sponsor it. Without the generosity of Datsun, the game would be struggling; they took over sponsorship of the sixty-overs games about five years ago and they've been very loyal since.

Sponsorship is at last on the increase in South African cricket, but I'm worried that it's not enough. I'm not speaking on behalf of myself, because I have a regular income from various sources, but I believe it's vital to hold on to our best players. The standard will drop if they go abroad to secure their financial future – and who can blame fine cricketers like Ken McEwan, Brian Davison and Barry Richards for making more cash from playing in Australia's Sheffield Shield? The best South African cricketers need the stimulus of Test cricket to realise their potential, but for the time being, they need commercial stimulus. In the past, many cricketers have made great personal sacrifices to play in the Currie Cup – they don't get a match fee, after all, only expenses, and they have to spend a fair amount of time away from their families.

I remember my former Springbok colleague, Jackie Du Preez telling me that he'd spent ten successive Christmases away from his family. Now professional sportsmen accept things like that, but it's different for amateurs, lacking at present the chance of playing Test cricket. We need more sponsorship in South African cricket to avoid our best players being scattered all over the world. Why else would Barry Richards find himself playing club cricket in Holland? With televised cricket now catching on, I would like to see the South African Cricket Association do more to attract sponsors. The big companies would get their free advertising and the players would also benefit.

In England the attitude to sponsorship is much better, probably because cricket is a professional sport there and the administrators realised eventually that the game would die unless it got regular cash transfusions from outside. At county level local advertisers pick up the bill for match expenses, in return for free plugs over the public address system, and billboards advertising their wares round the ground. I think that's a mutually satisfactory deal and no county cricketers I know complain. And every county secretary is delighted; it means more work for the club's administrative staff, but if sponsorship keeps the professional game going, it's all to the good. At Test level, Cornhill Insurance have given the English players a marvellous deal – in 1977, they were getting £250 per Test appearance and now, after Cornhill took over the sponsorship of Tests in England, that's gone up to £1,400. I hope that the expertise of the English administrators will be tapped by the South African Cricket Association if we ever return to Test cricket.

Team selection is also much better in England. In South Africa, we tend to chop and change all over the place, instead of keeping a settled side. English counties play up to forty games a season in all competitions, yet they very rarely use more than twenty players. On the other hand, I remember one season when Transvaal called on twenty-one players for just a few Currie Cup matches! In South Africa the provincial sides can draw from about ten first division clubs who play weekend cricket, but this vast range means that players often don't know whether they face a last chance or that they'll be dropped after a bad performance in the Currie Cup.

Now I'm all for keeping a cricketer on his toes, but it does his confidence no good if the team gets revised every game. In England, a county player will get a good run to establish himself before being dropped; the club realise that he wouldn't be on their books if he wasn't a good player, so they show faith in their own talent-spotting ability as well as the cricketer. In the Currie Cup, it often happens that a good player is replaced by an inferior one; with this in mind my side, Natal, resisted the temptation to make wholesale changes last season. We finished third in the Currie Cup, which wasn't all that great an achievement, yet our second side won the 'B' section. But our selectors realised that the players in the first team were better than those in the 'B' section and kept faith with them. In the end, you should always back class and I hope Natal's policy will soon pay off.

Barry Richards has the same views as me on the subject. We often discussed the selectorial whims of South African cricket and when Barry took over as Natal's captain, he asked the selectors to stick to the best players. The previous season, Natal had finished bottom of the table, but this time, they walked away with the Currie Cup, playing superb attacking cricket. The players knew they wouldn't be dropped for taking a chance with bat or ball and they responded magnificently to Barry's vote of confidence in them.

Talking of team selection, I'm sure many cricket experts have sat down and picked their South African eleven to play Test cricket again if the ban was lifted tomorrow. That's a subject the players wonder about as well, but here's my team.

JIMMY COOK

PETER KIRSTEN

BARRY RICHARDS

GRAEME POLLOCK

ALLAN LAMB

CLIVE RICE

MIKE PROCTER

TICH SMITH *(wk)*

ALAN KOURIE

VINCE VAN DER BIJL

GARTH LE ROUX

I hope I'm not being too immodest in including myself! Some of these names might not be too familiar to English readers. Jimmy Cook plays for Transvaal and is not only a fine player, but also a brilliant outfielder. I've chosen my Natal team-mate, 'Tich' Smith ahead of Transvaal's Ray Jennings, because he's a better batsman and just as good a keeper. Alan Kourie would be the solitary spinner, apart from Procter's occasional off-spin. Kourie plays for Transvaal, bowls left-arm and he's a competent batsman and keen fielder.

Among the others who would be in the shake-up are Denys Hobson (a very fine leg-spin and googly bowler), Eddie Barlow, Henry Fotheringham (a very consistent batsman for several seasons now) and Kepler Wessels (if he decided against qualifying for Australia).

71

All we need now is the chance to show our paces. I'd hate to think that all the young cricketing talent in South Africa is going to be confined to the Currie Cup and English county cricket for another decade.

6

Batting

There is no doubt in my mind that cricket is a batsman's game. I like the idea of these blokes running up and bowling at me, while I try to thrash the ball out of their reach, all the while consoling myself with the thought that the bowlers will get tired before I do. A batsman's life expectancy is longer in first-class cricket because it's not so physically demanding as bowling, particularly pace bowling. Men like Cowdrey, Graveney, Bobby Simpson and Boycott have prospered in their forties without being very athletic. To me batting is just like golf, it's a case of just going out there and playing. You don't have to be physically fit to be a batsman, but you must be *mentally* fit. I once got a century in seventy-six minutes against Surrey at Cheltenham when I'd had a late night. I was not what you could call fully fit, but I was able to recognise a half-volley when I saw it.

I suppose I prefer batting, because it's psychologically easier for me. My type of bowling is hard work, and I can see the day ahead where I concentrate more and more on my batting, so perhaps I'm preparing myself subconsciously for that. It's a great feeling to dominate the bowlers. I was lucky enough to be brought up on hard, bouncy South African wickets and my philosophy of attack stems from that. In South Africa, the batsman knows that although the ball may swing a little, it won't do much off the seam after the first few overs with the new ball, so a batsman can settle in and concentrate on taking the attack apart if he's in the mood.

Batting also attracts me because I look the part more as a batsman than a bowler. For all my faults as a batsman, at least I'm orthodox. My favourite shot is the cover-drive, and my skill in that direction is the direct result of hours of practice as a boy under the wise guidance of my cricket-master, John Saunders. I used to hit every ball to leg, until Mr Saunders took some ciné shots of me. When I watched myself on film I could see where I was going wrong. After that we concentrated on my off-side shots for hour after hour until I'd got them grooved and organised. I can hear him now: Get that left foot forward, get the bat up and bring that downswing through quickly. After that, I was on my way – I hit five centuries for my prep school in one season at the age of twelve, including an unbeaten double. Without John Saunders, I would never have got anywhere near that tally of runs.

I suppose my batting has got looser over the years and I blame one-day cricket for that. You reach the stage where you just have to score runs and any method will suffice. Now I find great difficulty in leaving balls alone in three-day cricket, because it is very difficult to change your style of play from one day to the next. In the one-day games you've got to be alive to the situation all the time as a batsman; you have to work out where the runs can be picked up. Sometimes you make the right decision and get the boundaries, on other occasions, your luck's out and you look a fool. There was the match against Warwick-shire in the Sunday League which should have been won by me; we needed three runs, with three balls to go, plenty of wickets in hand and me on strike. How could we possibly lose from that position? Bob Willis was in the middle of a very good final over and as he ran in to bowl the fourth ball, I thought, 'If I can whack this through the off-side, I can settle for two and that's just one to get with two balls left'. I should have just played it calmly away and settled for a single. But the ball moved in off the seam and bowled me. I couldn't see where I could have got a boundary because all the fielders were back on the fence, but I was very annoyed at myself for not winning the game when we started the final over, needing just six runs to win. After I was out, we only managed one off two balls, and I blame myself for losing the game. But it's hard to see how else I could have played; I batted in my usual fashion to get us into a winning position. I simply selected the wrong shot for the appropriate delivery.

The one-day brand of cricket has certainly altered the style of English batsmanship. They play a lot further away from their body than they used to when I first came over. Men like Boycott, Graveney and Cowdrey played straight and accumulated, but now the modern ones have to play at balls from outside the off-stump and work the ball down to third man for a single. We all end up playing bad shots because the situation demands risk-taking but it's very difficult to get out of those bad habits when you play three-day or Test cricket.

When I bat, I always try to play in my natural fashion, which means attacking the ball and trying to hit the bowler off his length. But I am playing more defensively now against the genuinely fast bowlers. We're going through a period of high pace and I tend to get on to the back foot a lot more than I used to against the quickies. I'm not a very good hooker, so I go for the cut or the pull if it's dropped short. The helmet gives me extra confidence, even though I've never been hit on the head at any stage of my career. There's not much chance of the cover drive against the really fast bowlers, because they just don't bowl half volleys, and if they do they're so quick that you're often beaten for pace. I think that the faster a guy bowls at you, the less chance you have of making a proper shot at it. I've never been frightened of fast bowling, but it does make you wary. All the batsman can do is hope the quick bowler gets tired; then you can punish him if he gets wayward. But if you're playing against the West Indies you're never going to get any respite from the unrelieved fast bowling. But we can't complain too much about that because that's how they win their matches, and who would be brave enough to break a winning formula of four fast bowlers?

With so many quick bowlers around, there's a growing tendency to make up one's mind about a particular shot before the ball is bowled. I know I play by numbers many times, especially in limited-overs matches; you have to grab a split second advantage, otherwise the ball's on you too quickly to adjust the stroke. Sometimes playing by numbers works, like the occasion against Essex in the Sunday League at Chelmsford. I walked outside my leg stump to one ball from John Lever and crashed it through the off-side for four, and for the next ball I decided to hit him behind square leg. The ball duly arrived, I was already in position for the shot and it went sweetly for six. But that system doesn't always work. Once, against Somerset, I was attracted by the short leg-side boundary, walked in front of my stumps, gave it the old heave-ho, missed and was plumb lbw for 99.

One of my main weaknesses as a batsman is that I do get carried away with the intoxication of playing shots. I tend to want to score runs faster than is necessary at a particular stage of the game; I know the side need me batting for a long time, but I have a habit of trying to get a lot of runs in too short a time. I don't seem to have the patience to hang around waiting for the bad balls, so I'm always going to give the bowler a chance. I won't change my style of batting when I'm getting near to a hundred. I can't understand why so many batsmen go into their shell when they approach their century. If you allow nerves to get at you when you've got so many runs on the board, you're giving the advantage to the bowler. The bowlers should be the nervous ones as they run up to bowl at you – they should be thinking, 'God, where's he going to smash this one?' If I think it'll win us the game, I'll declare with my score on 99. In the 1979 English season, I had a run of scores in the nineties, all of them made in fast time. There were various reasons why I didn't reach three figures: the side needed quick runs to make up for time lost through rain, I was rushing because I was trying for the fastest hundred of the season, and I was playing my normal game anyway. I didn't worry too much when I missed out and it all came good in the final county match of the season, when I scored 100 in fifty-seven minutes. During that golden spell, I just felt I could do nothing wrong with the bat, after a fairly disappointing season. I felt supremely confident – a vital part of any batsman's make-up.

As a general rule, a batsman should always play the way that suits him best, but even first-class cricketers forget that sometimes. I certainly did that in a Gillette Cup match against Surrey at the Oval. We were chasing 200 and at one stage we'd lost five men for just over 50. I'd been out of form and I played ultra-cautiously by my standards. I was itching to give it a whack but I was too conscious of the lack of batting left. I even went as far as leaving three balls in a row outside my off-stump! 'I mustn't get out,' I kept telling myself and I batted for thirty-four overs for 50-odd runs until I played my first really attacking stroke. I went to pull a bad delivery down the leg-side and was caught on the square leg boundary. We lost the tie whereas if I'd played my normal game, we would have had a better chance of winning.

I can always tell if a batsman's out of form – he plays the ball too soon. The later you play the ball the safer the shot, but a player who's struggling wants to get the feel of the bat on to the ball and he pushes at it almost before it has landed. That's why out-of-form players are regularly dismissed by such balls as full tosses and wide deliveries. You get stuck in a groove and almost dread having a crack at the ball. I normally continue playing shots even when I'm out of form, because I feel that you've got to back your own judgement in the long run and have confidence in yourself.

I'm not a great believer in net practice for myself when I'm short of runs because I feel the middle is totally different from nets, so I just concentrate on treating each ball on its merits during my innings. Easier said than done, though. I still get myself out too often. The best way to bowl at me is to get me fretting against a well-set field and tight, accurate bowling. I get very irritated if I make a good shot, only to be robbed of a deserved boundary by a brilliant piece of fielding. That's when I start thinking 'That's four runs they owe me, I'll have to make up for that now,' and I begin to strain at the leash.

I'm a terrible watcher when it's my turn to bat. My best position is number four or five, but I prefer just to walk out after picking up any old bat, instead of sitting watching the bowlers. But, as captain, I have to watch our batsmen at Gloucestershire because I'm expected to give opinions on their abilities if requested by the cricket committee. Batting always looks harder to me when I'm in the dressing-room, waiting for my turn. I find it easier once I'm out there. I don't really mind which bat I use, as long as it has a short handle, because the long handle ones just feel uncomfortable. But I do fret when I'm sitting with my pads on – mind you, I've never played regularly in a very strong batting side, so I don't have to wait all that long for a bat!

Although I play some rash shots on an easy wicket, I never get bored at the crease; I love it, but I do find it hard to concentrate. The more difficult the situation, the easier I find it to concentrate. I remember what a terrible headache I had after I'd batted for the first time in first-class cricket. It was for Gloucestershire against the South African tourists at Bristol in 1965. Barry Richards and I didn't bat very long – about ninety minutes to put on just over 100 – and we came together when the score was 30-odd for 4. But my head was splitting afterwards because of the concentration involved.

One other occasion when I was very conscious of concentration was in the knock when I equalled the achievement of C. B. Fry and Don Bradman in making six hundreds in a row. I didn't know a thing about their record until the press started blowing it all up after I'd got my fourth. I was never aware of any extra tension when I went out to bat that day for Rhodesia against Western Province. After all, at 5 for 3 there was enough work to be done, without bothering about personal records. Early on in that innings, I was dropped at slip by the opposition skipper, André Bruyns; he juggled with the ball three times and I could have hugged him when the ball fell to the ground. I went on to make 254 – my highest score in first-class cricket, and the four hours I batted meant it was my longest innings. It was a great day for me and among the most treasured messages I received was one from the Rhodesian Premier, Ian Smith.

My batting in that 1970-71 season remains one of the happiest memories of my career. Nothing I've ever done as a bowler could match it, and to this day I still get more pleasure out of making 100 runs than taking a stack of wickets.

All the really satisfying innings of my career have been when the side has been up against it and we've had to struggle through. Anyone of ability can get an easy 100 on a flat wicket against a tired attack, but a batsman who gets his side out of trouble has the double pleasure of personal and team satisfaction. I enjoyed my 90-odd which helped us beat Sussex in the Gillette Cup Final. We'd lost three wickets very cheaply and although it was important I stayed in, I recall how everything felt just right that day, so I could also play my natural game. When Mike Buss dropped a couple short, I pulled him for two sixes over mid-wicket and the crowd's roar and the sight of the ball disappearing were sweet sensations. In the semi-final at Worcester that year, I'd also played well. We'd lost two early wickets and I was dropped first ball off Brian Brain, but I concentrated hard, got 100 and played as well as I could have played at any stage of my career. In both games, the tense situation and the fact that I was nervous brought the best out of me.

Some of my most satisfying knocks have been the ones against the clock that helped win the match for my side. There was the game against Yorkshire when Geoff Boycott set us a fairly difficult target. The wicket was flat but we were 30-odd for 3 at one stage. By teatime we needed 180 off the equivalent of twenty-seven or twenty-eight overs, and I said to Tony Brown that it would be a good idea to have a crack at it, because I felt fairly good. Boycott put John Hampshire on to bowl immediately after tea to tempt us and we took about forty off his three overs, leaving us about five an over. Chris Old and Tony Nicholson came back to bowl, the Yorkshire lads started moaning among themselves, and we won easily. I scored a century and I'll never forget the look on the face of Arthur Milton when he arrived back at the ground, after picking up my car from the garage where it had broken down. He just couldn't believe we'd won. But you never know whether you can win until you try.

Of course, I've enjoyed the fast hundreds in my career,

but on many occasions they've been simply a case of 'hit and hope'. A lot of people raved about my 154 not out against Somerset in a Benson and Hedges Cup tie. I got my last 50 in twenty minutes, aided by some dubious tactics which left poor Kerry O'Keefe having to bowl the last over – a leg spinner expected to keep it tight in the last over of an innings, with a batsman well set, and on a small ground like Taunton! What chance did Kerry have? With those short boundaries, if you aim to hit a slow bowler over the top and you middle it, nine times out of ten it will go for six. It was one of those days when everything went right. Kerry didn't bowl all that badly, but a good length leg break in a limited-over match is a hittable ball.

In terms of value to the side, I suppose one of my best knocks has to be one of 22 not out, with the injured Barry Richards at the other end. That helped the Rest of the World beat England by two wickets at Leeds in 1970 and when Barry joined me, we were still 40-odd short. Far too often, cricket experts are dazzled by fast scoring or huge individual scores and they start bandying around the adjective 'great'. As far as I'm concerned, an innings can only be described as 'great' if it wins or saves a match for the side when there's a hard struggle on.

The three finest batsmen I've seen were Barry and Viv Richards and Graeme Pollock. Graeme was a murderer of bowlers when his eye was in; he didn't care all that much about footwork, but his superb eye and long reach compensated for that deficiency in technique. He never seemed to play a defensive bat/pad shot, his bat was always in front of the pad. When going well, he would play cover drives to balls pitching on the middle stump. He played late, so that he was making the shot with his eyes almost directly over the ball. He had a fantastic Test record and there's just no telling what he would have done if his international career hadn't ended at the age of twenty-six. Since then he's scored thousands of runs in the Currie Cup, he's tightened up his leg-side technique and in my view, Graeme's still a great player.

Viv Richards is dazzling, exciting, with a shot for every ball it seems. But he'll give the bowler a chance because he hates to be tied down and he has that touch of arrogance most great players need. That great confidence stems from an awareness of his magnificent ability, but it means he'll often try something flamboyant to show what a wonderful player he is.

If I had to select one batsman to play for my life, it would have to be Barry Richards. He was such a complete all-round batsman that if he felt like it, he could bat all day and the bowlers couldn't do a damned thing about it. He would make it look so ridiculously easy – there was simply no technical weakness in his game, off front or back foot. Because of our friendly rivalry over the years, Barry seemed to concentrate more against me than other bowlers and I hardly ever got him out. And when Barry Richards decided to concentrate, it was a case of game, set and match to him.

Graeme and Viv would at least give the poor old bowler a chance. Viv's bias towards the on-side always encouraged me to bowl round the wicket at him to try to get the ball to swing in to him. I've managed to get him lbw on occasions when the ball has swung as he played across the line. With Graeme I had even more of a chance, because my natural inswing would cause the ball to leave the left-hander in the off-stump region. I've often picked up Graeme in the slips or had him caught behind the wicket, though mind you, that's normally happened after he's got 100 against his name!

The best bowlers I've ever faced? Very difficult to answer that easily. Michael Holding has been the fastest, Andy Roberts the most dangerous because he varies his pace so well, and manages to bowl two types of bouncer:

a fairly slow one that deceives you into playing too soon, and the other a fast ball straight at the throat that really whistles through. Dennis Lillee has been a great, brave, resourceful fast bowler over the last decade; he never seemed to waste a ball at his peak. And what a great Test match performer! The hardest spin bowler to pick was, for me, Johnny Gleeson of Australia; he didn't spin it very much, but I could never really tell which way it was going.

I've got no doubts over the best ball I've ever received – it was the perfect off-break from Fred Titmus of Middlesex. We were batting on a slow turner and the first ball he bowled to me was tossed up a little higher. It started off around the off stump, then it swung gently away towards first slip. I thought it was going to be a nice juicy half volley and I launched into the off-drive, only to discover it had pitched in some rough and came back in between bat and pad to take the off-stump. A classic delivery from a very fine bowler.

As the years go by, I find myself thinking about how I can alter my batting. I'm reasonably happy with my technique, thanks to John Saunders and all those coaching films in my boyhood, but I must tighten up a little, while maintaining the ability to attack the bowling. I don't think I'll ever be a four-hour hundred man in the Boycott mould, but at the same time, if I can manage to score hundreds at the age of forty like him, I'll be very well pleased.

7

Bowling

Even though I regard myself as a batsman who bowls, I'm generally regarded by the public as a bowler who bats; I suppose that's because I used to be a fast bowler, and the sight of someone tearing in off a long run and scattering the stumps is exciting and spectacular. I know youngsters particularly worship sheer pace, rather than other facets of cricket, so if I've helped to fire the enthusiasm of some of them by running long distances with the ball in my hand, I'm quite happy.

But I have not bowled consistently fast since about 1973. Injuries, particularly a bad knee, and the general wear and tear of playing cricket all the year round have taken their toll. I can still slip in a few quick ones if I'm feeling good and the wicket encourages me, but primarily I'm now a swing bowler. I've never really known just how fast I was or how you compare yourself to others in the same category. But it used to be a great feeling to bowl a good player when his bat was still on the down-swing.

I have been a very lucky cricketer in many ways but especially when it comes to my bowling action; to say the least, it's unorthodox, but many other youngsters would have had it coached out of them by well-meaning cricket masters. John Saunders left me alone, told me that if it felt right, I wasn't to worry. I got used to people telling me that I was a coach's nightmare when I bowled fast. I've often been told that I bowl off the wrong foot, yet that's untrue. If you watch closely, you'll see that I deliver the ball just *before* my left foot hits the ground, unlike the orthodox right-arm fast bowler who pivots on the left foot at the moment of delivery and then bowls against a straight left leg and a braced left side. I've got a faster arm action than most quick bowlers, so I let go of the ball fractionally earlier than most bowlers, but that's totally different from bowling off the wrong foot. One day I got so fed up with people telling me about bowling off the wrong foot that I tried it in the nets – I ran in, bowled off the right foot and nearly broke my back! I agree my action isn't textbook (with my open-chested delivery, I'm basically an inswing bowler) but it feels right to me, and surely every cricketer should do what comes naturally?

I just don't know how I developed my action. I only started bowling to get involved in the game, after I'd grown too tall for the job of wicket-keeper. So if my prep school wanted a spinner, I volunteered; if they wanted an opening bowler, I wanted the job. Then I opened the bowling for Natal Schools and South African Schools, but I wasn't very quick, and far too wild to be much use to the side. But I was getting stronger and stronger and when I played for Gloucestershire Seconds in 1965 I was quite successful as a quickie. But I was not prepared for the shock of opening bowling for South Africa against Australia eighteen months later! To this day, I can't work out how I managed to improve my bowling overnight; strength, fitness and keenness had a lot to do with it, I suppose. Throughout this period I was conscious that my bowling action was a little unusual but it wasn't till after my first Test that I received concrete proof. I went to the pictures, some news film came on which dealt with our victory over Australia, and when I saw myself bowling on screen, I just couldn't believe it!

Of course, I wish I had a better action because I reckon I lose half a yard. I'm basically a swing bowler, and I'm fortunate in that respect because a lot of bowlers can only make the ball go off the seam rather than through the air. Having said that, I wish I'd had the smooth run-up and body action of a McKenzie or a Sobers. They had it all – an explosive delivery after just a few strides to the crease, a classical side-on position and a wonderful follow-through. With a bowling action like theirs I reckon I could bowl quick till I was fifty, but I had to make do with the Mike Procter model rather than the Rolls Royce. I'm often cricicised for what seems like an excessively long run-up but those critics don't realise that this is the only way I can generate speed. I need to get momentum from a long run because I get no speed from my body action. It's quite simple: the faster I run, the quicker I bowl. Whenever I've tried to bowl fast off a shorter run, it's taken more out of me because it means I have to concentrate on a higher amount of physical exertion in a shorter period of time.

Some bowlers need long run-ups, others don't. Guys like Andy Roberts and Len Pascoe take comparatively short run-ups, while men like Michael Holding need to run a long way just to get their rhythm going. I don't agree with those who say that Holding is just as quick off his short run, he only does that to boost the over rate. Slow over rates are a problem for fast bowlers, and the West Indians don't help by waiting at the bowling crease until the ball's returned to them. You just can't do that in county cricket, your club would be fined consistently for slow over rates. I'm like other opening bowlers in that we walk straight back to the mark when the ball's delivered, but I do take my time while walking back, partly to get my breath back and also to work out what my next ball's going to be. The length of my run-up varies quite a lot; I mark out fifteen paces and then I walk back as far as I feel like running that day. It all depends on my physical condition, what the wicket's like and whether it's warm. Sunshine definitely helps quick bowlers, it gets them loose and they don't have to worry about muscle strains if they're warm.

I use my long run-up for psychological reasons, as well as the fact that it helps me bowl quicker. I'll never change my field on the way back to my mark, or if I'm standing at the wicket – I'll wait till I'm at the start of my run-up. I'll pause, bark out a few instructions and try to let the batsman think there's some devious subtle plot afoot. I might then get him wondering why I've suddenly changed the field and as I'm running in at him his concentration won't be exclusively on me, he'll possibly still be thinking about the fielders. As a batsman myself, I believe that they think more about their game than a fast bowler; a quickie basically runs up and lets it go while a batsman has to deal with varieties of bowling and placement of shot. So any kidology I can think of to unsettle the batsman is worth it, in my opinion. I want him to have a seed of doubt planted in his mind as I'm running in to bowl.

I think subconsciously fast bowlers try even harder against great batsmen. After all, it's a case of attack at both ends: the bowler knows he must blast the batsman out, and for his part he resents being tied down and wants to assert his authority. That's always an exciting contest. I like the way the Australians play the game with their fast bowlers – they'll get through their overs fairly quickly and attack all the time. People like Lillee often go for over a hundred but they do get wickets. They're philosophical about the nick for four to the third man boundary, because they reckon that eventually four slips and two gullies will catch one of those nicks. When I bowl against men like Viv Richards, I attack – there's no point in trying for line and length, because he'll just smack them all over the place. I just try to keep my head up, let him think I've got him sorted out and hope he'll over-reach himself and play a rash shot. A lot depends on the state of the game and the condition of the wicket, but in recent years I've taken myself off if there's little chance of me getting out a great player. There's no shame involved in that, if you think someone has a better chance of dismissing him.

I wasn't always so sensible. I used to get really narked if I got smashed all over the place, going in even faster off a longer run, bowling more wildly and getting hammered even more. I once bowled for Natal against Graeme Pollock from just after lunch until close of play and he kept hitting me out of sight as I got madder and madder and tried to bowl even faster. I finished up with 0 for 148 and next morning, I couldn't get out of bed, I was as stiff as a plank. Served me right, I should have concentrated on Graeme's off stump and tried swinging the ball away from the bat, instead of tearing in at great speed.

I don't mind getting hit as long as I've got a chance of taking wickets. It's more important, in my opinion, to take wickets consistently, rather than bowl economically yet look unlikely to bowl a side out. It doesn't matter if the wickets cost a bit, because the object of the exercise is to get the opposition out as soon as possible. Men like Tom Cartwright used to say you'd bowled well if so many runs had been scored off so many overs. I can't understand that philosophy and it hasn't helped English cricket much. That's why Ian Botham is a better bowler than Mike Hendrick. Botham knocks over batsmen regularly while Hendrick always looks impressive, beats the bat often, yet never gets the wickets he seems to deserve. Hendrick is a magnificent line-and-length bowler who just runs up and tries to hit the seam. On some dodgy county wickets he's almost unplayable, but in Tests he's never taken five wickets in an innings. Botham, on the other hand, will experiment – he'll try an outswinger, then an inswinger, a bouncer and a slower ball in one over. He'll grin and say 'Good shot' if you smash him, but he'll come back for more and buy his wickets.

I've played with some English bowlers who knew exactly how many runs had been hit off their bowling after they'd sent down twenty-odd overs. It was easy to tell then how many wickets they'd taken: very few, because they were too obsessed with nagging accuracy and getting the batsman into a defensive groove. That means bore-dom for the spectator while the bowler is satisfied with his day's work, even though he never really looked like getting many wickets.

I expect to give away runs when I'm bowling because I'm attacking; even more so when I'm bowling my off-breaks. How I'd love to bat against my off-spinners! They seem to take an age to come down, and I'd be trying to hit them out of sight all the time. I bowled off-breaks at school but I didn't pick them up again until I was established in county cricket, and I saw that my days as a fast bowler were drawing to a close. It would be like losing an arm to give up bowling, so I started working at my off-spin, with amusing and sometimes rewarding results. When the ball is turning on the last day in England, I find I can lure some batsmen to self-destruction with my high, slow, looping off-spin. I can spin it quite a lot, but perhaps I give it too much air. I get panned on flat wickets but perhaps that's because I try too many variations. I can never really work out how a class batsman gets out to my off-breaks, and if anyone blocks them, I stand there and give him a mouthful. I tell him he can't bat if he can't score off me – even more so if I suspect he's playing for himself and not his side. A few 'not outs' can make all the difference to a player's average at the end of the season and I get really narked if I think a bloke is playing for his average.

Although I've got very het up sometimes while bowling, I've never really set out to hurt a batsman – except once. We were playing at Northampton and I was in the middle of a very bad spell with the bat. I took six wickets on a very flat track on the first day and at the close I was about 5 not out, determined to build an innings. That night, I was due to go to a party with David Green, Hylton Ackerman and Colin Milburn, but I decided on an early night. I felt I owed it to the club to be seen to be concentrating on my batting, even though a night out has never affected my form the next day. Anyway, after two halves of lager I went back to the hotel, had a meal and turned in for the night. Next morning I was as fresh as a daisy, pulling the legs of Messrs Milburn and Co; I had a net, felt really good and took the first over. I blocked the first two balls and padded up to the next, which turned out to be a straight ball and it knocked out the middle stump. I didn't realise it at the time, but both sides knew about my early night, and the Gloucestershire dressing-room was in hysterics as I walked back. David Steele was fielding at short leg, trying hard not to reveal his amuse-ment; unluckily for him I saw him burst out laughing as I walked out. I wasn't aware that all the Northants lads were in the same state and I vowed to exact revenge on Steele in their second innings. When he batted I dug one in at him first ball – he played forward and it broke his arm. He was out of action for over a month and I was appalled at myself. I had got so wound up about my bad batting and the fact that I'd looked a fool padding up to a straight one that I'd over-reacted.

Since then, I've never tried to injure a batsman. But intimidation is a different thing; after all they have a helmet, a bat and various protective clothing to help cushion the blows, so what's wrong with keeping the batsman on his toes? I agree that some fast bowlers get carried away a little at times, but the umpires (especially in England) are pretty strict on intimidation. You can't take away the element of physical danger, but there are only certain occasions where a bouncer is used. I won't bounce someone if I know he's going to leave it alone, because that's simply a waste of effort. The game is now more dangerous, mainly because we're going through an era of fast bowling. Within a decade, there's no reason why the pendulum won't have swung the other way and spin bowlers be back in fashion. I hope so, because that would mean more overs per hour and more attacking cricket. But this reliance on speed has proved the trump card for the West Indies. They're now world champions because of their fast bowlers, and can anyone really blame them for playing to their strength? Wouldn't England do the same? What about the Bodyline Series in 1932/3 against Australia? England used four fast bowlers most of the time, and there wasn't much spin used by them in the series.

Many right-arm fast bowlers I know don't like bowling to left-handers. I'm quite happy about that, because my natural inswing normally gets them fending at the ball leaving their bats. Having said that, I do find that left-handers play and miss a lot. Right-handers play the ball a lot more, because, in my case, the ball's coming in to the right-hander, but when the ball is leaving the bat, the left-hander is bound to struggle to make contact, especially if it's a quick delivery. Often I'll bowl around the wicket to a left-hander to lessen the swing, because it's doing too much. But swing's a funny subject, because there are times when I can bowl just outside the left-hander's leg-stump in the hope of getting the ball to swing across him, and it won't deviate at all. Then if I bowl it on his middle and leg, it'll still swing too far away to the slips and he won't need to play a shot. The same thing happens with a right-hander sometimes. If I bowl middle and off at him, the ball often goes down the leg-side, so I'll try to bowl a little wide of the off stump, only to find it just goes straight on! There's a very thin dividing line between getting the ball exactly where you want it and bowling a harmless delivery. A lot depends on the conditions and how much the ball is swinging. That's something that varies from day to day and I've never known what's likely to happen. I hear first-class cricketers say things like, 'It's really going to swing around today', and I'd love to know how they work that out. Often they're proved totally wrong.

Sometimes the ball just starts moving for no apparent reason on a clear summer's day. That's what happened when I got my hat-trick against Hampshire in the Benson and Hedges Cup semi-final in 1977. It all looked very dramatic on TV as I took four wickets in five balls; the media kept going on about Procter blasting them out with sheer pace, but that wasn't so. I did it with swing bowling and I still can't work out why the ball started swinging for me on a flat wicket when it hadn't swung for anyone else all day. We were really up against it: all out for 180, facing batsmen like Richards, Greenidge, Turner and Jesty. Well, after a couple of overs I noticed the ball was swinging for me, so I changed to bowling round the wicket to ensure the ball didn't swing too much. With the fifth ball of my fourth over, I bowled Greenidge. With the second ball of my fifth over, I had Richards lbw and the same thing happened to Jesty next ball. For the hat-trick ball, I got the angle just right to bowl John Rice; with the ball swinging so much, I wanted to pitch it up to make it deviate in the air. I also wanted it just outside off-stump so that it would swing into him. It worked a treat and he was clean-bowled, off-stump. Next ball, I was convinced I had Nigel Cowley lbw, but Tom Spencer turned me down. Can't complain, though, and I wasn't just pleased with the hat-trick – I took myself off after six overs to save myself for the end and I had to bowl the penultimate over with Hampshire needing just 9 to win and Andy Roberts hitting dangerously. I bowled a maiden at him and Brian Brain finished it off with three balls to spare, giving us victory by seven runs. One of those days when everything went right.

I've had five hat-tricks for Gloucestershire – four of them in county cricket, and the fifth the Benson and Hedges one. All of them have happened when the ball's been swinging around a lot and most of the wickets have been taken from round the wicket. When the ball is swinging I've got little chance of an lbw because the ball is doing too much, but when I go round it's just about the right line and length for an lbw. In fact, twelve of those fifteen hat-trick wickets have been lbws. Two of them were all lbw hat-tricks – the first at Southend in 1972 against Essex. The wicket was fairly lively and the ball swung a great deal. I got Edmeades and Ward out in successive balls and I conned Keith Boyce out for the hat-trick. I think he was expecting a bouncer first ball because he'd bowled a few at me in my innings. I pitched it well up and Keith was on the back foot, half expecting the bouncer, and he was plumb lbw. The second lbw hat-trick was at Bristol in 1979 against Yorkshire. In overcast conditions, I bowled round the wicket and got Lumb, Athey and Hampshire. The crucial thing here was that I managed to bowl the last two deliveries straight and the swing did the rest.

Don't ask me how I manage to get things right on certain days and not on others. There are days when it all just seems right and you're in rhythm. There was the time when I took 7 for 13 against the Indians at Bristol. I didn't swing the ball at all, I got my wickets by using the seam and making it hit the pitch to run it away to slips.

That's unusual for me; in fact four of those seven wickets stemmed from catches behind the wicket. Normally, I get my wickets with lbws or I clean bowl the right-hander, because of my natural inswing. Then there was the time when I took fourteen wickets in the match at Cheltenham against Worcestershire; I didn't bowl very fast because Brian Brain was injured and I knew I would have to do a lot of bowling. I kept hitting the seam and our lads kept catching the snicks and it all worked out well. I got an early boost on the second morning when Glenn Turner was out to a loosener. I just ran up, turned my arm over and it bounced a little more than he anticipated and he edged it to slip. That kind of thing puts a spring in the step of any bowler and they collapsed from 80 for 1 to 111 all out.

Strangely enough, my best bowling performance in statistical terms came when I bowled off-spin. I took 9 for 71 for Rhodesia against Transvaal and eight of them were taken when I changed to off-breaks. The wicket was turning a lot on the final afternoon and I managed to pitch it in the right spot most of the time. We ended up winning with ten minutes to spare, so in the context of the game it was a very satisfying performance. But I wouldn't brag about it too much.

I'll keep on bowling my off-breaks because they're useful to the side when the wicket's helping me; apart from that, they keep me involved in the game. There's no doubt in my mind that if I had been a specialist batsman like Barry Richards, boredom might have become a problem as the seasons went by. As an all-rounder, I can get two bites at the cherry. But it's not really a game for bowlers, you know; in my experience the best deliveries don't usually get wickets, they normally bounce too much or move off the pitch too sharply. Many great deliveries are too good for the batsman's reflexes and he can't get near them, and it's no consolation when he looks down the wicket at you, nods and says, 'Well bowled.' To be a bowler, you've got to have a philosophical turn of mind because your day only comes a few times a season. Then it's up to you to capitalise on your luck and the favourable conditions.

8

Captaincy

I'm often asked how I manage to combine the roles of all-rounder and captain. 'Isn't it too much of a strain?' they ask. I honestly don't find it so. I'm not the greatest theorist or worrier in the world and I tend to act on hunches or impulses. Early on in my captaincy career I learned one thing that's stood me in good stead since: it's not the end of the world if you make a mistake. You can only try your best, follow your tactical inclinations and get your side behind you all the way. I like to make decisions for others and I find captaincy a genuinely creative challenge; it's nice to be able to help youngsters along in their careers, in the same way that I received help from experienced men like Jackie McGlew when I first came into the game.

Of course, the strains of captaincy are there, even for someone like me who finds it easy to unwind after a day's play. I captained Rhodesia for five years and I've been in charge at Gloucestershire since 1977, so I've had my ups and downs as skipper. Sometimes I've wished I hadn't been stuck with all the hassle of committee meetings, treating the players as individuals with their own distinct problems, and getting the flak from the press if the team's not doing as well as it should. But it soon passes. I tend to bottle things up and work it all out in my own mind – a weakness I agree. Perhaps I should discuss problems more with the side, but at the same time I've always believed that the captain should lead from the front. He should be an inspiration. He owes it to the rest of the team to put on a match-winning performance whenever he can. His example should get them thinking 'If the skipper can do it, then so can we'. The captain shouldn't confess his doubts and frailties to the rest of his side, nor should he go on about his own injuries and form problems. Many times I've gone into a match less than fully fit without telling my side, because if the team has complete confidence in the captain they'll be better players because of that confidence. I feel a captain's example should be a positive one all the time, even if it means he doesn't communicate opinions and doubts as much as he should to his side.

A county cricket captain always has to keep in touch with new rules and think of ways of applying them for the benefit of his team. That's been a particular dilemma in the hundred-overs limit games in the county championship; many times we've been faced with a flat wicket, a good batting side and the knowledge that our comparatively weak bowling side could be in for a hammering. My reaction to that is to rush through overs whenever possible, for the simple reason that this tactic will give us more time to get a positive result once the first two innings are out of the way. I recall one match in particular against Glamorgan in 1977 when David Graveney and I bowled our spinners at a rate of twenty-eight overs an hour. In the end we lost the match, but at least we'd given ourselves some elbow room.

I've often been surprised at the way experienced English professionals don't use their hundred-overs allocation. Time after time, they took an age to set up a platform for a big score, then find they've run out of overs and still have too many wickets in hand. Three examples from recent years demonstrate this. At Southend in 1977 Essex made 294 in their allotted overs on a good batting wicket, but they only lost 5 wickets in the process. Good hitters of the ball like Mike Denness, Neil Smith and Ray East didn't even get a bat. We got a lead of 40-odd and secured maximum batting points with some sensible, unselfish hitting by Alastair Hignell and David Shepherd, and when I took a hat-trick in their second innings, they were bowled out for 147 and we won by 5 wickets. The crucial part of that victory, however, was the way in which Essex had wasted their advantage on the first day. Another 40 runs would have been difficult – but we'd made the most of our opportunities.

At Guildford in 1978 Surrey only made 268 for 6 in their hundred overs and they should have made a hell of a lot more; when we batted, we lost the first three batsmen for 38, but we still pressed on. The wicket was beginning to take spin, I chanced my arm, hit 154 in two hours and we got a precious lead of 60-odd. Our spinners John Childs and David Graveney bowled them out and we scraped home by two wickets with the ball turning all over the place.

At Bristol in 1979, we led Leicestershire on first innings by 70-odd because we were happy to lose more wickets than them in chasing the runs. They scored 314 for the loss of just four wickets on the first day, while we lost eight wickets in establishing a lead that won us the match. On a rain-affected wicket, we bowled them out for 134 in the second innings and if we'd had to get 150 on that wicket, we would really have been struggling. But we'd done the right thing earlier in the game by getting our runs quickly when the going was easier.

The stereotyped nature of the forty-overs John Player Sunday League games leads to headaches for a captain, especially when rain reduces the allocation of overs and you end up getting the slide-rule out to calculate scoring rates. But I'm quite happy to play these kinds of matches – the public enjoy them, there's a definite finish and it fills the grounds. Not every county captain I've known has shared my philosophical attitude to the John Player League – Brian Close, for one. In 1970 we were playing Yorkshire and they found themselves involved in an ideal position for a win – just three wickets down, needing 6 an over, a tall order in those days but still possible. The word came out from Close in the dressing room: 'No chance of winning this one, lads – just get some batting practice.' I couldn't believe it. It took Close some time (and a sacking from Yorkshire) before he got used to playing forty-overs cricket. Nowadays no side would ever dream of playing that way.

My happiest memory of captaincy must be the 1977 season in England, when Gloucestershire came so close to winning the Championship, the competition that means more to the players than any other. We managed to win the Benson and Hedges Cup that season and we were still in with a chance of the title right until the final afternoon of the last championship match against Hampshire. It was my first year as Gloucestershire captain and, looking back, it was amazing that we came so near to a double success, because we didn't have a great side; indeed, there've been better Gloucestershire sides since then. But our secret was that indefinable one – team spirit. Everybody worked so hard for each other that we just wouldn't accept the word 'defeat'. We played positively, only drawing six matches out of twenty, and at last the fickle Bristol public got behind us.

By the time we played Hampshire in that final match, I was convinced we were going to win the title, even though I knew we didn't deserve it in terms of skill. Even the omens were right – one of the lads found out that all the Gloucestershire side that won the title back in 1877 wore moustaches, so the obvious thing for us to do was try the same. In the centenary year since we'd last won the championship, we all started to grow moustaches in the last month of the season. How could the fates deny us? Well I don't know what they were doing but Gordon Greenidge brought us back to the world of reality. He made a brilliant 94 as they reached their target of 271 in just over three hours, with eighty minutes to spare. Looking back, I think I made a tactical error by not playing it tight enough. I was so totally convinced that we were going to win that game that I attacked in the field all the time, with most of the overs coming from the spinners. But we didn't look like champions in that match and we had to content ourselves with third place, behind Kent and Middlesex.

In a way, that marvellous season has worked against us, because the hopes of our supporters and the cricket writers were raised by Gloucestershire playing above themselves for a season. I was embarrassed by the headline writers calling us 'Proctershire' when everyone else in the team was giving so much; it meant we had a lot to live up to and we've struggled in recent seasons to do ourselves justice. But at least we've played attractive cricket. Unlike other counties, we bowl our spinners a lot, we have several batsmen who are happy to give the ball a wallop and we try our best for a positive result. I can honestly say that Gloucestershire play cricket the way I like it to be played.

I do get frustrated at other captains in the county championship. The attitude of most of them seems to be, 'Right, we're not going to lose, and if we happen to win, that's a bonus.' They don't seem to want to try to make sure they can win. Now I know the captain has responsibilities to his players, to the committee and to the public to make sure his side is not a soft touch but I do think some captains lose sight of the fact that we're there because the public pay our wages. I don't like drawn games – the side that plays the best cricket should win in an ideal world. Under my captaincy Gloucestershire have lost a few games we should have won, but at least we've usually tried for a positive result. There was the match against Surrey at Cheltenham when the first day was washed out. The Surrey captain, Roger Knight, wasn't over-keen about my suggestion that we should unofficially limit the first two innings to fifty overs each. I persuaded him to give it a go and when he won the toss, he put the onus on us by asking us to bat first. We led by 50 on the first innings and they needed 267 to win in three hours; our spinners bowled thirty-three of the fifty-four overs and they won by just one wicket. I bowled the last ball: it went just over the top of the middle stump, and the last pair scampered to a bye to win the match. It was a great game of cricket, but I was sad that we'd lost because we'd made most of the running throughout. A tie would have been a fair result.

There are times when I can't do a thing about forcing a positive result because the wicket is so slow and gives no encouragement to the bowler. Such a game was the one at Bristol in 1979 against Warwickshire; that was the worst kind of match, where I knew only one result was possible from the second morning onwards: a draw. Dennis Amiss got a double century, more than 1,300 runs were scored in the three days and everyone got bored stiff as just 14 wickets fell. I did my best to liven up the proceedings by trying for the fastest 100 of the season (I failed – 92 in thirty-five minutes) but I would have been far happier with a nought and none for plenty as a bowler if there had been any way of getting a decent game out of it.

In games like the Warwickshire one, I get very bored. I tend to let things slide and the game just meanders on. A weakness in my captaincy, I agree. I always like something definite to aim for, and I get very frustrated sometimes when I think we're the only side that's trying to get things moving. The batsman's patting back half volleys at you, he's playing for his hundred and forgetting about the clock and his captain hasn't bothered to tell him to pull his finger out. At such times I feel very sorry for the public.

I won't have players in my side who simply play for themselves. Geoff Boycott, for example, would never be in my team because I don't think he considers the team's immediate needs enough. Now I admire his dedication, his fitness and his ability – I saw his superb century in the Gillette Cup Final against Surrey in 1965 and nobody can ever tell me this guy hasn't got some great shots. He proved the same thing in Australia against Lillee, Thomson and the rest in several one-day internationals. It's just that Boycott doesn't use his strokes all that often. I get on reasonably well with Geoff but he's always struck me as a guy who doesn't really enjoy playing the game of cricket but loves batting. To him batting is the ultimate and the game is incidental to that.

I'll never forget a Sunday League match at Cheltenham when for the first time I can recall I was tempted to bowl Brian Brain and myself straight through our allotted eight overs; normally I keep us back for a final effort near the end of the innings, but on this occasion Yorkshire got terribly behind the clock at the start. After the first ten overs, they'd scored just 6 – Boycott didn't even try to take singles, he kept patting the ball back to me, saying 'Well bowled' and I kept answering, 'Well batted', while pinching myself to see if this really was happening. I ended up with 3 for 6 off my eight overs, unbelievable figures for the Sunday League and I hadn't bowled all that well, either. We won by seven wickets and Geoff Boycott lost that match because he played for Geoff Boycott, not for his side. No wonder Yorkshire eventually dropped him for some of the forty-overs games.

Boycott would have been a tremendous asset to the South African side if we'd played more Test cricket. With all our stroke-makers we would have needed someone to hold up an end and accumulate runs, while Pollock and Co. blazed away at the other end. But it's different in the England team because he puts pressure on the other batsmen. I felt sorry for Tavare and Woolmer when they were dropped against the West Indies – they followed Boycott's example and tried to grind down the pace attack. They did as well as anyone could have expected, but they were dumped while Boycott (who played the same way) stayed in. Mind you, I don't think he should have been picked again for England after he dropped out for personal reasons in 1974. Three years later, he comes back, scores runs against the Aussies – and he's rewarded with the vice-captaincy of England for the winter tour of Pakistan and New Zealand! To me, that's wrong – the game should always be bigger than the individual. People keep making excuses for him, that he's been brought up the hard way, and that he's made the most of a limited batting ability. Well, I disagree – he's got more batting talent than men like Mike Gatting or Brian Rose and he should use that ability more often.

Men like David Shepherd are the ones I'd always have in my team. Big David was never the most athletic of men – you could call him comfortably built – but he was a great trier. I'll never forget his fielding in the Benson and Hedges Final when we easily beat Kent, a much more talented side than ours. David threw his bulky figure all over the place in the field and so saved many runs. As a batsman he always played for the team; he'd do anything the skipper asked. He was the kind of man you always wanted to do well, because he epitomised all that's best about cricket. He never cared about his batting average yet he made so many effective contributions for us over the years, particularly in 1973 when we won the Gillette Cup. That year he rescued us many times in the earlier rounds after bad batting by the top order. I particularly remember a superb 72 not out that won us the second match against Surrey, after Geoff Arnold had gone through the earlier batting like a dose of salts. Then there was the time at Taunton when Shep did all he could to keep our championship hopes alive; on the final morning, we were just 104 ahead with only four wickets left but Shep guided David Graveney through to a big stand. Shep made a courageous 142 not out and Somerset were left to get 272 in three hours. We bowled badly and they won a great game by five wickets with eleven balls to spare. But it was Shep who gave us a chance of victory with a controlled innings and the delight on the face of his team-mates when he walked in undefeated told its own story about the affection we had for him. Little did the public know that we'd all been up late the night before, having a few drinks and a good old sing-song with Shep out front, giving us a rendition of his favourite rugby songs!

Phil Bainbridge is another man who knows the importance of playing for the team, and he found that out in a match against the Indians. Young Phil played very well indeed to reach 81 not out, on the brink of his maiden century in first-class cricket – then I declared. There wasn't a murmur from Phil, because he knew that we needed time to bowl out the Indians if we had a chance of winning the match. Phil had guided us from being in danger of following on, but I declared 80-odd behind. It all turned out right in the end, because they crumpled in their second innings and we became the first county team to defeat the Indians. The crowd soon forgot the names they'd called me for denying Phil his moment of personal triumph.

In the modern game, the captain is very much in the firing line and tempers can snap on occasions. I'm not exactly blameless in this respect and sometimes I say things in the heat of the moment that I regret later. But there are two incidents from my career as captain where I honestly believe I was blameless and they still both rankle with me after all these years.

In my first year as Gloucestershire's captain, we were playing Worcestershire at Cheltenham. They didn't have a twelfth man for some reason and ours fielded for them throughout a morning session. Now Jim Foat was a magnificent fielder in the covers or the deep – one of the best in England at that time. But unfortunately Jim dropped me when I lapped the ball down the hill, always a difficult place to field at Cheltenham, because the ground slopes away quite sharply. I was out just before lunch and sat having a rest at lunchtime when Norman Gifford, the Worcestershire captain, came over to me; he suggested that Jim Foat hadn't tried all that hard for the catch. I was furious. I told Gifford, 'If that's what you think, you can do without our twelfth man.' So they fielded with ten men until another player was summoned from Worcester. It had become a matter of principle to me, it was very unfair to suspect that Jim Foat had cheated.

I felt the same way in November 1972 in South Africa, when I believe my Rhodesian side were the victims of some sharp practice by Lorrie Wilmot, the Eastern Province skipper. To this day I am convinced that justice was not done. Rhodesia would have won the Currie Cup if the opposition captain had not walked off the field with his team over a dispute about the number of overs left. And even more amazingly, his action led to his team sharing the trophy that season!

To recap, Lorrie Wilmot set us a target of 324 to win in four hours, including twenty overs in the last hour. I told our team we were going for the runs, because that's the way I believe cricket should be played. We all played well and then came the crucial drinks interval at 4.45. Just before that an over was bowled and I noticed my opposition captain talking to his bowler and one of the umpires, who was asked if this coming over was the first of the twenty overs. The umpire (Chris Sweeting) said he thought so, but just before play restarted, his colleague (Ian Forrest) held up one finger to tell Sweeting that there was one over left before the drinks interval – and then the twenty overs would start. I was batting at the time and it seemed rather confusing. I was under the impression that the start of the twenty overs had been signalled, but I had not been officially informed about this and I knew that the laws stated that they could only start after the drinks interval. During that fateful over, umpire Forrest told me not to worry, that the matter would be sorted out during drinks. When that arrived, the scorers were told that the first of the compulsory twenty overs was to start immediately after drinks. Lorrie Wilmot and I were then called over by the umpires and told the situation; Lorrie wasn't too happy because he thought there were only nineteen to go, even when I told him that the batting side as well as the fielding side has to be told when the twenty overs are to start, and that hadn't happened.

Anyway, Lorrie appeared to accept the situation and as far as I was concerned, the umpires had made a slight mistake which had been quickly rectified during drinks. Come the end of the nineteenth over, we needed just six to win with four wickets in hand; I was still batting and deep in conversation with my partner, Paddy Clift, when I looked around to see the Eastern Province team walking off! I was astonished, and after the umpires had called 'Play' once or twice, we walked back to the pavilion, convinced that Rhodesia had been awarded the game. This was confirmed to me by the umpires and I thought that was correct. I then called my players together, told them we were going in to have a drink with the opposition and to steer clear of discussing Wilmot's tactics. It all went off well and Wilmot and I shook hands afterwards.

A few days later, came the bombshell. The South African Cricket Association reversed the umpire's decision, called it a draw and took the ten points away from Rhodesia. I couldn't believe it, it seemed such a stupid decision because it appeared to sanction a side walking off the field if it disagreed with an umpire's decision. Law 46 was clearly on our side: 'All disputes shall be determined by the umpires and if they disagree, the actual state of affairs shall continue.' But after discussion, the umpires *had* agreed on their decision and they informed me of it: that the twenty overs were due to start *after* the drinks interval. And the rules of the Currie Cup clearly state that hours of play are determined by the home state and that the umpires apply them accordingly. In this case, with play ending at 5.45 p.m., drinks were taken at 4.45 and Lorrie Wilmot was well aware of that. The rules also state that if the umpires are in position before 4.45 p.m., or if an over is in progress at 4.45 p.m., that over shall *not* count as one of the twenty. Obviously I based our batting strategy round the fact that we had an over to come and I felt desperately sorry for the crowd, who were deprived of a great finish. Lorrie Wilmot clearly felt he was acting in the best interests of his team, but I felt he had a duty to cricket as well; he should have bowled the final over under protest, given the crowd their finish and then tried to get the result reversed.

So we ended up with seventy-nine points in the Currie Cup, behind Transvaal, Eastern Province and Western Province, who all had eighty-four points. We were robbed of the title and it's still a bitter pill to swallow.

I've often wondered how some of the captains I've played under would have reacted to that incident. I'd like to think Jackie McGlew would have handled it the same way as me; he was the first captain I played under and he taught me such a lot. In my early days I was awe-struck by the man who had been a legend in South African cricket and who managed our schools side to England in 1963. For the first few years in the Currie Cup, I called him 'Mr McGlew', even after I'd become a Test player! His tactical ability was first-rate. I remember a match where he totally outwitted Peter Van Der Merwe of Eastern Province. We were struggling when McGlew came in to join David Pithey and the pair took us from 120 for 8 to 250. That left Eastern Province needing just over 200 to win and with Eddie Barlow hitting a rapid century they seemed to be coasting home. But then McGlew posted two silly mid-offs to Eddie who seemed to resent this. He heaved at the next ball and was bowled; Eastern Province then collapsed and we won the game. That piece of tactics taught me the importance of attacking captaincy and the use of psychology.

I played Test cricket under two very successful captains, Ali Bacher and Peter Van Der Merwe. They were both similar in outlook, with Ali the better batsman and perhaps the more dynamic influence, but without being disrespectful to either, they led sides that were so powerful they didn't really need a captain. The luck was with us most of the time in those two series against the Australians and I would have been interested to see how Ali or Peter would have fared as the Australian captain, with all the breaks going the other way. But Ali in particular was such a fine skipper that he would have done well with even a weak side.

It's impossible to name the greatest captain I've known because you take a little from all of them and try to assemble an identikit leader. Gary Sobers was certainly the greatest inspiration I played under and during that 1970 Rest of the World series, the side could take great comfort from the fact that he would always pull out a great innings or a dynamic piece of bowling if the chips were down. He wasn't a great tactician because he expected his players to perform in his style. It was a shame that he came to county cricket at a late age, because he would definitely have won trophies for Nottinghamshire in his prime and with a sound pair of knees. But there's no doubt in my mind that he was the greatest all-rounder cricketer I've seen and his attacking style of captaincy was right up my street.

Ray Illingworth, Gary's opposite number in that 1970 series, was of a totally different style. He was a mean, nagging captain in the field with a great memory for a batsman's weakness. He had the characteristic 'give them nothing' philosophy of most Yorkshire cricketers I've known, but he was a high-class tactician whose own performances seemed to get better under the responsibilities of captaincy. Every Illingworth team was behind the captain. He fought hard for his players' interests and defended them over niggling matters like expenses and having to attend meaningless functions where his tired players would have to put up with a lot of ear-bashing. And any captain who gets John Snow to bowl his heart out must be a little special. Mind you, Illy could try it on with you in the field. He was always moaning about something. Once I walked back towards the pavilion when I thought I'd been caught and bowled by Jackie Birkenshaw; but Jackie called me back, saying it was a bump ball. But Illy told him off, saying he should leave the decision to the umpire and moaning loudly about the bloody overseas players who were ruining the game. I told him that if he wanted my wicket that badly I'd walk off.

Mike Brearley was in complete contrast to Illingworth.

A cool, unruffled guy, he had a terrific record as England captain. I know a lot of cynics point out that he didn't have all that much to beat because Kerry Packer had creamed off a lot of the world's best players, but that's not Brearley's fault. You can only beat those who're put in against you and he did that often enough. Unfortunately he wasn't worth his place in the side as a player. He's a far better batsman than he's given credit for – safe, brave and a good evader of fast bowling, with the ability to drop his wrists on nasty lifters – but he was never one of the top six English batsmen. Only in England do you have a system whereby the England captain is picked and the ten other players are later selected to balance the merits or failings of the captain as a player.

I suppose it's all to do with tradition, but for all that, there's no way that Mike Brearley would have ever captained South Africa or Australia. Having said that, I think Brearley should have been used to give Ian Botham much-needed experience before Botham took over the England captaincy. As a good player of fast bowling and a first-rate tactician, Brearley would have held his own against the West Indian quickies in England, while Botham learnt his trade as vice-captain without the full glare of press interest on him. It was a little unfair to expect a bloke of twenty-four to captain his country against the world champions with no previous experience. It would have been easier for Botham first time round in the Caribbean; there the English press would have banded together, killed all those boring stories about the Botham waistline and supported him. In a wet English summer, when there's no cricket to write about, Fleet Street will seize a topic and never let it go. In the 1980 English season that topic was Botham, his form and his weight. If Brearley had still been skipper, Botham would have fared better. After all, he's got the job for as long as he wants, because there's no one else who is a certainty to play for England for the next five years. It all seems to have happened rather quickly for Botham, though, and he didn't help himself all that much in the 1980 season. He thrives on hard work as a bowler but his back injury and the bad weather gave him little chance to keep his weight down. He should have trained harder and looked after himself a little bit more.

One of the reasons why Botham will retain the England captaincy for as long as his form and interest in the game lasts is because there are just no contenders for the job. He's an absolute natural as a cricketer, a high-class all-rounder by any standards, but that doesn't mean he'll make a good Test captain. But as long as county teams are captained by men like Mike Procter, he'll have no rivals for the England captaincy. That may seem oddly self-critical, but I firmly believe that as long as overseas players captain teams in England the problem of the England captaincy will remain. Very few Test-class players get the chance of experiencing leadership at county level because the Procters, the Rices, the Barlows, the Davisons and the Turners block the way. That can't be right for the health of English cricket, which relies a lot on a successful Test side. Surely the more experienced English captains there are in county cricket, the better the chances of a successful national side? Apart from that, I believe a county side needs a captain running the show twelve months in the year, rather than from September to March. He's needed for fund-raising and public relations exercises on behalf of the county during the winter to whip up new members. He's not much use to his county if he's playing in the Currie Cup or the Sheffield Shield.

9

Physical Fitness in Cricket

At this stage in my career I have to face the facts and come to terms with the physical strain my body's taken by playing professional cricket twelve months a year since 1967. I chose this profession, and there are no grouses from me about it, but playing so much does take it out of me at times. The last time I *didn't* play cricket for a month was in 1975, and that was only because I was recuperating from a serious knee operation. I've now come to terms with the fact that I'll never be as quick as I was in the early seventies, and thank heaven that I can bat a bit and get by with my off-spin. I've told Gloucestershire I can't bowl quick any more and they've accepted it and they realise I won't be trying to blast too many batsmen out in future.

But following my knee trouble in 1975, every day I walk out on to the field is a bonus. Without the brilliance of a Bristol surgeon called Keith Lucas, I probably would have been finished at the age of twenty-nine. The trouble started earlier in the year when I was having a game of touch rugby in Rhodesia. I was wearing cricket boots, I did an inside break and my studs got caught in the turf. My foot went at one angle and my body at the other. My right knee stiffened up and I went to see a specialist, and he even gave me a chance of playing for Rhodesia against Western Province the next day. But next morning I was on crutches and I then had an operation to remove the cartilege. It took a long time to get right, I couldn't put my full weight on it when I was walking. I wasn't allowed to bowl and after I'd batted, the knee would swell up alarmingly. Eventually the specialist said I would have to have some sort of transplant and I went to another specialist in Johannesburg who told me the same thing. In March 1975 I came back to England, where Keith Lucas operated on me. Even now, I think it's amazing. He cut my knee open and reconstructed the cruciate ligaments by taking a tendon from the inside of my leg and placing it inside the knee. That stronger tendon could then take the weight which I would exert on my knee when bowling. It was a fantastic feat of skill and I started training at the Bristol City Soccer club under the supervision of our own physiotherapist, Les Bardsley. I was lucky because I trained a lot with Dave Rogers, a guy who'd had the same trouble, yet he was back playing regularly for Bristol City. I tried hard not to feel sorry for myself. After all, I still had my batting and if Dave Rogers could make it back, well so could I.

I was making good progress towards full recovery throughout the summer of 1975 and everybody kept telling me I had to slow down. But we'd got to the semi-finals of the Gillette Cup and I desperately wanted to play. I felt fit enough and wanted to pay back something for all the loyalty and kindness I'd experienced at Bristol since my injury. I persuaded the club to let me play against Lancashire at Old Trafford. I was ahead of schedule and I thought I'd proved my point, as I bowled my first seven overs tightly and well. I bowled one very good over at Clive Lloyd, beating him four times out of six – and I slipped in a bouncer for good measure. That felt good and when the crowd started jeering me,

113

I got carried away. I can remember running up to bowl at Clive Lloyd and then I was lying on my back in the middle of the wicket. I was carried off the field, the Lancashire physio told our chairman I'd never play first-class cricket again and to complete a black day for Gloucestershire, we lost the semi-final with three balls to go.

I wasn't aware of the physio's gloomy forecast, I was simply sitting in the bath, cursing myself for trying too hard. But I always thought I'd play again and when Keith Lucas diagnosed a strain on the knee, I was comparatively happy. All I needed was complete rest and Keith said I'd be able to play again. He was right and I have total faith in that man. He's now semi-retired but I still go and have a check-up with him at the start of every English season. The funny thing is that Keith doesn't know much about cricket and he never saw me bowl until we won the Benson and Hedges Cup in 1977. He sent me a letter of congratulations and pointed out that he couldn't work out how my good leg stood up to the hard work involved in bowling, never mind my suspect one!

Now I sometimes have trouble with the knee, and on other days it's fine. I've learned to live with it, even when it takes me ten minutes to get out of bed after a long bowl the day before. The trouble is caused by the fact that my bizarre bowling action means most of my weight is placed on the right knee after I've delivered the ball; normally, a right-arm fast bowler's left side and knee take the strain as he pounds the left foot down before delivery but in my case, I deliver the ball early and run through my left leg. So my right knee is braced to take the strain. Nowadays I wear a brace if the knee's playing up and it does help. But from now on, it's just a case of being sensible and realising I'm not twenty-one any longer.

A fast bowler always has niggling injuries during a season, and I usually come back to England with a few left over from South Africa. I always have shoulder trouble in the first few weeks of the English season, and put that down to the cold. I get back-ache as well, but that's an occupational hazard. A fast bowler is usually fully fit for the first few weeks of an English season – then it's a long round of visits to the treatment table. He has to try to ignore the nagging injuries in areas like the groin, the shoulders, the side and the ankles; he just mustn't think too much about pain because his captain needs him to bowl. Often a fast bowler is not aware of an injury till he's standing at the bar or having a shower; you get so wrapped up in the game that it's easy to dismiss little twinges, only to find out that they are serious.

In my experience, batsmen have a different attitude to the pain barrier. They're much more precious; so many of them seem wary of getting hit when a good technique and footwork would keep them out of harm's way. Too many of them seem happy to retire with a finger injury, rather than bat on. Not many of them show the guts of Gehan Mendis, who batted with a broken finger for Sussex in the Gillette Cup Final against Somerset's Botham and Garner. I wonder how many top-class batsmen have experienced the prolonged pain of someone like Bob Willis or Dennis Lillee? Both of them have had bad series of injuries during their careers yet they've battled through operations, setbacks and worries about their future, and they've picked up more than 400 Test wickets between them. Lillee was still on pain-killers at night when he played World Series Cricket; they were to combat pain from a back injury he's carried since 1972! That kind of attitude takes guts and mental resilience.

A fast bowler has to be a bit of a masochist to enjoy his trade. Think of it – slaving away under a hot sun, with your feet killing you, as you run full-pelt up to a batsman who smashes you out of sight! Yet the next day we turn up raring to go through it all over again. There must be easier ways of earning a living, surely? But you just grit your teeth and get on with it, even though you know it's going to be a hard session. A successful fast bowler needs guts, dedication and physical fitness. I shudder to think how many miles I run for Gloucestershire during a typical county season: we play in four competitions and on average, we're in action five or six days a week over a four-month period. In all competitions, I bowl about 1,000 overs, most of them off a thirty-five-yard run-up, six times an over. I daren't work it out, because if I knew the total, I'd put my feet up for a week!

The need for physical fitness has dawned on first-class cricketers in recent years; quite simply a fit cricketer is a better player, because he can still concentrate on his game, instead of being distracted by considerations like, 'God, I'm tired, how long till close of play?' I suppose it's easier to reach physical fitness in a warm climate like South Africa, than it is in England. In my country, there's an outdoor philosophy – it's a sports-mad nation. Things are a little more easy-going in England, where more is taken for granted and the facilities aren't so good. Having said that, the change in attitude towards keeping fit among English professionals has been remarkable in my time. Until recent years, you would never see a professional running round the pitch before the start of play; at the start of the season, there'd be a little circuit training in the gym and that would be it for the rest of the season. You'd rely on nets and match practice to keep you fit.

We've been ahead of most counties in Gloucestershire when it comes to pre-season training and our physiotherapist, Les Bardsley, is a man who knows about these things. He's played professional soccer, managed a Football League side and worked with Gloucestershire for twenty years, so we've got a head start over other counties. When Brian Brain joined us from Worcestershire at the age of thirty-five, he told us he never did any special

116

training, all they did was play cricket at Worcester. We soon changed his ideas, although I respected the fact that he must have known what was best for him after playing for so long. It's amazing how he manages to bowl so many overs – he smokes and drinks, doesn't do any training at all between the start of September and the end of March, yet he turns up and bowls through a season. There's not an ounce of fat on him, he's deceptively quick and hardly ever wants to stop bowling during a match. Yet he's become an even better bowler because he's had to train with us. If he'd done more of that earlier in his career, I think he would have played for England. He's got the ability.

Derek Underwood is another of the old-style English players who had to change his ways. I'll never forget the look of horror on his face in the first year of World Series Cricket when he was told to run round the ground. He'd never had an injury in nearly twenty years of cricket and he relied simply on bowling to keep himself fit. But he had to do it, because you can't make an exception for him.

Ian Chappell really put the Aussies through the mangle in the second year of World Series Cricket. He hired a scientist to check their fitness levels and they went through a really tough training programme. But it worked, and the Aussies were a better team in that second year of WSC, and fitness must have had something to do with it. The West Indies had the same attitude during WSC. They hired a top Aussie physiotherapist to get them into shape and they were so pleased that they use him all the time now. Look at the England team under the direction of Bernard Thomas – they've become a really good fielding side in recent years, and that's the kind of encouragement every bowler needs. It's a great boost to your morale when you've bowled a bad delivery, only to see one of your fielders stop the ball being smacked for a boundary.

World Series Cricket also helped toughen me up. I soon

realised that competition was going to be fierce, so I worked hard at the physical fitness programmes. I enjoy the feeling of being physically fit, I like to be over-tired, and I can't train gently. I feel that if you're trying to get fit, the best thing to do is get on with it and stop going through the motions. I run about four miles a day (always on soft grass, because a hard surface jars my knee) and this helps build up my leg muscles and tones up my knee. I like to push myself, and make sure I have to run to a certain spot, so that I have to run to get back. If you simply run round a park, you can stop any time you like, as soon as you get bored or tired. But if you set yourself a target, you just have to get back the way you came. I don't really enjoy the physical aspect of running, but it's good for you and it has to be done. I enjoy squash very much; I play it a lot, and like the way it tones up the reactions and sharpens up the footwork. I play golf, and when in South Africa, I play tennis with my wife, Maryna. She usually beats me, but then she was our country's number two player and represented us in the Federation Cup!

Physical fitness is the one aspect of cricket where a player at any level can improve himself by a great margin. A club cricketer or a schoolboy will probably become more proficient in the technical side of the game if he gets proper coaching or graduates to a higher standard of match play, but he'll certainly be a better player if he gets fitter. He'll be able to run those quick singles, take two to third man, or keep wicket all day without losing his concentration through fatigue, or answer his captain's call and come back with a fast spell of bowling near the end of the day.

118

10

Coaching

No matter how talented the cricketer, he'll never get to the top if he doesn't work at his game in the crucial years of his boyhood. I believe that the vital years of a player's development are between the ages of eight and eighteen; that's when he should be learning the basics of the game, trying to work out what facet of cricket suits his particular talents and, all the while, working very hard. That initial grounding is vital, and as the Rhodesian coach for five years I realised early just how important it was to get the coaches thinking along particular lines right from the start.

I soon saw that the problem wasn't so much to do with coaching the youngsters, as telling their teachers what to look out for. I shudder to think how many promising cricket careers have been ruined by a well-intentioned but misguided coach or cricket master. Not enough cricket masters are put through coaching classes themselves and they often end up hindering the development of promising youngsters. Fundamentally, coaching has to be as natural as possible: you mustn't stick rigidly to the rule book and natural ability should always be channelled in the right direction. I was lucky in getting proper coaching almost before I could walk and I wonder what would have happened to me if my cricket master had tried to coach me out of my unusual bowling action. But he saw that it wasn't putting any strain on my physique and he left me alone to do what came naturally. But without the basic coaching, I wouldn't have prospered as a cricketer. I had it drummed into me at prep school, so by the time I went to Hilton College I was into a well-coached groove with my batting.

I was very lucky in many respects, not least that I was born into a sports-mad family. My mother was a provincial tennis player and my father played for Eastern Province against Wally Hammond's MCC side in 1938. My brother, Anton, also played for Natal in the Currie Cup, a couple of times in the same side as myself, a proud day for our parents. My father, not surprisingly, was my first coach and he drilled the basics into me almost as soon as I could walk. How many times must he have watched my bowling action, been tempted to do something about it, yet resisted? He knew that a bowler with a textbook action and nothing else isn't much of a bowler.

By the time I was eight, I just wanted to play cricket for South Africa. School studies were irrelevant as I worked hard at my game. When I went to Hilton College, I played squash, hockey, rugby and tennis for the first teams but cricket was my true passion and I slaved away at the nets for hour after hour. The advice of Jackie McGlew was invaluable when I toured England in 1963 with South African Schools, and when Barry Richards and I went back to England to play for Gloucestershire Seconds we practised and practised to get the feel of English wickets. In those days the club was so hard up that they'd switch off the hot water when the first team was away, so Barry and I had to endure endless cold showers on freezing English days after long sessions in the nets. Barry was no different to me in his attitude to coaching and practice; when he was on his own as a small boy, he used to spend

hours throwing a golf ball against a wall and hitting it
back with a cricket bat to sharpen up his reflexes. When
he became an established player, Barry made it look easy,
but he had to work very hard as a boy to gain that
mastery.

Even when I first played for Natal, I still spent an hour
or so a day in the nets. I'd remember the ones who'd turn
up, lark around for half-an-hour, then stroll off for a
shower, convinced that they'd done enough. In those early
days, it's a question of practice, practice, practice – and if
you're lucky, you'll have a coach who'll tell you how to
bowl the outswinger or why you're picking up your bat
wrongly. Now that I'm an established player, it wouldn't
bother me if I never had another net in my life. I know the
way I play, which shots are my strengths and which ones I
shan't attempt, and I just find net practice unrealistic and
no substitute for the real thing. I can get away with that
because I play cricket all the year round and if a guy feels
better for a long net, that's all to the good. But there's no
pressure in the nets and you don't get the chance to play a
particular shot unless your net bowlers are very accurate.

I find English players very much wrapped up in the idea
of net practice; I see them playing shots in the nets that
they'll never dream of playing in the middle. English
coaches look at the game differently from those in South
Africa and they start with the basic premise that defence is
more important than attack. Perhaps the wickets have
something to do with that, but in England they hammer
home the doctrine of getting the left foot to the pitch of
the ball, getting behind the line and leaving the ball alone
if it's going outside the off-stump. I've often wondered
how a great natural cricketer like Ian Botham managed to
slip through the system – it's refreshing to see an Englishman who attacks with the ball and crashes the bowlers
around when he bats. He plays like an overseas cricketer;
there are mini-Bothams all over the place in South Africa,

and it's exciting to be in a position to coach them through to realising their attacking potential.

Arthur Milton, that typically safe and solid English batsman, unwittingly demonstrated the different attitudes to cricket in his country compared to mine. When I first played regular county cricket I was a bit of a dasher as a batsman (I suppose I haven't changed all that much!), and early on, I got a fast 100 against Hampshire. A week later, I was in the process of sharing a big stand with Arthur and no doubt we were an interesting contrast in styles. Arthur was nearly forty at the time, full of cricket wisdom and a man I respected greatly. I'd got to the nineties in even time and, as is my wont, saw no reason why I should change my style of batting just because I was near to the three figure mark. I was out for 94 and afterwards Arthur said to me, 'When you're in the nineties, you get to your hundred in singles and it doesn't matter how long it takes.' Then there was the time at Chesterfield when we put on over 200 together; I'd come in on a hat-trick and it was going rather well. Then Edwin Smith, the off-spinner, came on and Arthur started playing him with exaggerated care. I kept coming down the wicket to him and saying, 'Come on Arthur, you've got to hit him over the top, he's asking for it.' It took half an hour to persuade him to show his shots against the off-spinner. Arthur was always of the opinion that it takes an English player six or seven seasons before he could confidently take his place in the England team, and I could never understand that. Now I know that seasoned, shrewd professionals know more than I do about the way England want their batsmen to play in Test cricket, but such long-term planning has always seemed safety-first to me. In other countries, you play for your country if you're good enough, no matter your age. The only reason why youngsters like Gower and Gooch got into the England side in 1978 was that men like Amiss, Woolmer and Greig had signed for Kerry Packer.

Otherwise they would have kicked their heels a while longer, waiting for the call from the selectors.

On the other hand, it must be said that experience of county cricket is essential for any overseas batsman. It's all very well to crash the ball on the up through the covers at Durban, but it's a different story when you have to bat against Mike Hendrick on a seamer's wicket at Chesterfield. Only Barry Richards has taken to it instantly, making over 2,000 runs in his first season with Hampshire – but he's always been a law unto himself. For the rest of us it's a case of doing away with an amateur attitude and trying to play like a professional. It's a great education and most of the world's top batsmen have played in county cricket in my time. But you can tell a South African player as he stands at the crease in county cricket; men like Lamb, Rice and Kirsten will play their shots while others are tied down. They may not make very many, but at least they'll get to 15 or so fairly quickly, compared to the time taken by an English player who's either out of form or just grafting away. It's all a matter of attitude, rather than natural talent; I believe there are plenty of English players who're blessed with the right attacking qualities, but they're not encouraged to go for their shots, unless it's near the end of the hundred overs or a Sunday League game. The South Africans, on the other hand, learn the basics on hard, fast wickets of even bounce, and they can grow in confidence, secure in the knowledge that they won't get their heads knocked off by a flier. Confidence is an important ingredient in any cricketer's make-up. It shows during a big match, you can see the ones who want the ball in the field and the others who'll do anything to avoid going for a high, swirling catch. And a confident batsman will want the strike because he fancies himself against the bowlers. Nothing wrong with that, provided it doesn't spill over into cockiness. The confident players like Botham are the ones who do themselves justice when the pressure's on.

I believe England's display in the Centenary Test at Lord's showed the basic defensiveness of their style of play. Greg Chappell's declaration was a very fair one, yet England approached the task determined not to lose. Only Gooch and Gower seemed interested in chasing the runs, they both got out, and then Boycott batted as if he'd set his heart on a century in the showpiece game – something to talk about, I suppose, in years to come, but it would have been nice to take the crowd into consideration after their frustrations earlier in the game. Kim Hughes did that. He wasn't bothered about playing for his second 100 of the match, he got out, forcing the pace for the good of his side. I suppose Australia could have closed the game down if England had even a chance of winning, but I still feel England should have made at least a gesture.

I kept thinking about all the kids that watched that last day's play; did they prefer the Kim Hughes way of batting or the England way? I hope for the good of cricket, it wasn't the latter. I know Test matches are serious occasions but we still have a duty to entertain and to inspire. I want kids to go home after seeing a great innings or spell of bowling and set their sights on emulating that. That's the great continuity of cricket, where memories warm someone on a cold day when net practice isn't going very well. That's how I felt when I watched Tom Graveney play so elegantly against the West Indies as I cleaned the West Indian gear in the Oval dressing-room in 1966. And today's players have the same duty to inspire as in any other era.

11

Cricket and the Media

Coverage of cricket by the press, television and radio is vital for the well-being of the game. We live in a world where so many social pursuits are clamouring for an individual's attention that cricket needs to get through to the public. The counter-attractions offered by the car, the cinema, the beach and family life all work against cricket and sometimes I wonder if the well-intentioned men who run the game are aware that it should be sold more effectively.

The public was left with a very sour taste in its mouth after the farcical events of the Saturday of the Centenary Test at Lord's. England had been playing Tests against the Aussies for over a century, yet Lord's still couldn't afford to cover the entire square when it rained, despite all the money that had been taken in advance bookings! The poor old umpires got it in the neck, even though they were simply applying the rules. So play didn't start till mid-afternoon, by which time the long-suffering crowd were really fed up. There seemed a lack of good public relations on that Saturday and the game was given the kind of publicity it could well do without.

I'm fairly philosophical about the way the media covers cricket. Broadly speaking, all publicity is worthwhile, because at least it gets people talking about the game. The next step is to get them along to the ground to watch. My barber in Bristol doesn't know about cricket, yet he talks about it to me because he's seen some of it on television or read about it in the papers. That's why John Arlott did so much for the game. In South Africa, we heard his voice over the radio as boys and he always seemed so knowledgeable. Years later when I met him and sampled some of his hospitality, I realised that he was all I had ever imagined: kind, intelligent, wise, with a fund of marvellous stories. In his commentaries he was always constructive, he never said anything malicious about a player, he'd always give him the benefit of the doubt. But the great thing about Arlott was that he reached out beyond the masses of cricket lovers throughout the world; his voice was so distinctive, his gift of description so great, that he attracted those who didn't really know or care about the game of cricket. In his own way, John Arlott must have recruited thousands of listeners to the army of cricket followers.

The same must be said about World Series Cricket. Now I appreciate the anti-Packer brigade will say I am biased but surely one of the merits of Packer was that he got people thinking about cricket? I know it wasn't too pleasant to see cricket dragged through the courts, but he caused a shake-up and made the administrators think again about how to sell the game to the public. The man in the street may not have heard of Mike Procter or Barry Richards, but pretty soon everyone knew about Kerry Packer, and as a result cricket was talked about more – and the various ways it could be improved.

Packer also ushered in a new era of television techniques; the camera work on Channel 9 was fantastic and even the BBC has adopted some of the little tricks, such as cameras at both ends and the easy-to-read statistical information about a particular player when he's caught in camera shot. Perhaps some of the slow motion shots were overdone, and perhaps the purists didn't like arrows on the screen pointing out square leg, etc. But those purists tend to forget that the majority of people watching Channel 9 were laymen and that these little gimmicks helped them understand the game. Perhaps some of the Channel 9 commentators got carried away a little – we kept hearing about 'the greatest shot you'll see all season' and so on – but I think the euphoria was a reaction to all the flak that had been flying around. We were told by the Establishment press that WSC was just a 'circus', that most of the games were rigged, that the fast bowlers had been encouraged to spill some blood and that the whole thing was a sham. For my part, I've never known more genuine or hard cricket in my career and the sweeping, unfair criticisms had the effect of binding us all tighter together. Everyone was so wound up to make it work that some of the commentators went a bit too far and over-praised the game and its players.

I was very surprised and disappointed that some well-respected journalists should have forgotten their Fleet Street principles and not given the other side a chance to state their case. It seemed to me that Fleet Street made up its mind pretty quickly over WSC; they knew where their bread was buttered and they decided to stick with the Establishment. Fair enough – but that didn't stop them slagging off a brand of cricket they didn't even bother to watch. It seemed astonishing for them to suggest that fifty of the world's top cricketers wouldn't try. Then, in the second season, they said that there was too much intimidation. Throughout the short history of WSC, Fleet Street kept pumping out the line of 'What price loyalty?' – yet how many of those same journalists would refuse an offer that doubled their pay if they worked for a rival newspaper? The issue was as simple as that. The Packer players had learned their trade in one sphere of cricket and now they were going where the money and competition were better. The same thing happens in the media world every day. But we couldn't win with Fleet Street.

The Packer issue also highlighted the fact that TV rights over cricket are a joke in England; the BBC has been getting away with cricket on the cheap for years. With the amount of coverage the BBC gets every year on cricket, I would have thought the deal must be worth at least a million pounds. The BBC gets every day of the Tests plus the highlights at night, five hours every Sunday in the John Player League and live action in various Gillette Cup and Benson and Hedges matches. That's about 400 hours of cricket in a four-month period. The Test and County Cricket Board should press for more cash for the game from the BBC; I know that the BBC has been going through a bad financial patch, but so has the game of cricket for a long time. The whole market may get very interesting in the very near future if the second ITV channel gets off the ground. The commercial branch will have pots of money to throw around and it wouldn't surprise me at all if the BBC lost cricket coverage to ITV. That would be a shame, really, because I think the BBC's coverage is first-rate, much better than anything ITV has accomplished. But money talks and the BBC seems reluctant to help out cricket, other than in its actual coverage. Why shouldn't the BBC sponsor a Test Match, for instance? Why leave it all to Cornhill Insurance?

I did a few cricket commentaries on Channel 9 and I found it highly enjoyable. It's not half as easy as I thought. You have to make sure you're not repeating yourself, talking too fast, telling the viewers about something that's not yet on the screen, you have to keep quiet at the appropriate moments, all the while listening to the director babbling away in your ear about which shots are

One of the problems of being a bowler/captain: even as I'm pulling my sweater on after an over, I've got to be thinking about whether the guy at the other end wants one slip or two (photo: Ken Kelly).

Sharing a quiet moment with Clive Lloyd and Viv Richards (photo: Ken Kelly).

Feet up in the Gloucestershire dressing-room, and while others watch the racing on TV, I find contentment in a cricket book. Note the slippers: bowlers need to take care of their feet in an English season (photo: Ken Kelly).

Waiting to bat. I don't lock myself away like some batsmen, but I do like to take a look at the bowling. David Graveney's doing the same, while Brian Brain's probably trying to persuade me to back his hot tip for the 3.30 (photo: Ken Kelly).

Thanking the Bristol crowd for their support on the last day of
the 1977 season, when we came so near to winning the
championship, only to lose to Hampshire (photo: Patrick Eagar).

Leading the Gloucestershire side off the field after I'd done the
hat-trick against Hampshire in the Benson and Hedges semi-
final, 1977.

Proof at last that I don't bowl off
the wrong foot. I simply deliver
the ball a little earlier than most
bowlers (photos: Ken Kelly).

Kerry Packer's World X1 in 1977.

Facing page: Playing the wrong shot to the wrong ball in a World Series Cricket match.

Right: 'Never mind, Dad, it's only a game...' (photo: Patrick Eagar).

Putting my son, Gregg, through his batting paces at Bristol (photo: Ken Kelly).

My wife, Maryna, in the days when she was number 2 womens' tennis player in South Africa.

With my family in Sydney in my first season with World Series Cricket.

coming up. It only deepened my admiration for Richie Benaud – he's the number one cricket commentator, in the opinion of most players. He's so calm and perceptive, with a shrewd insight into the way the game's progressing. He has the knack of anticipating dismissals and letting you know what the bowler's trying to achieve. To me he's totally unbiased and gives praise where it's due to any side.

I'd love to have a go at commentaries back in South Africa when I stop playing. Television's only been going for about four years in South Africa, but it's catching on strong and the cricket coverage is improving all the time. Coverage is limited to about an hour and a half of live action on the Saturday afternoons and then recorded highlights on Mondays. Lee Irvine does some commentaries and so does the former Springbok fast bowler, Neil Adcock.

I think a lot of professional cricketers have a rather jaundiced view of the media. They seem to forget that the guys in the press box have also got a job to do and many players resent seeing critical comments about their performances in print. They're not aware of the problems newspapermen and broadcasters face – many cricketers believe the correspondent is responsible for writing the headline over his report. Many times I've seen a player curse and throw the paper on the floor of the dressing-room without acknowledging that the reporter is entitled to his opinion or that the sub-editor back in the office has set the headline. And it's not the writer's fault if a sentence comes out wrong or a paragraph is missed due to an error in the printing works.

I find that the best way to deal with the media is to answer their questions honestly, to realise that most of the cricket writers understand the game (particularly in England), to develop a thick skin if things aren't going your way on the field, and to make a mental note of those who sell you short by publishing an off-the-record quote or a moment of indiscretion. I speak as I find and I've got no lasting grudge against anyone from the media world. We're all basically in the same boat together and I like to think we all want the game of cricket to prosper.

There's no doubt in my mind that Fleet Street has a large say in the selection of the England team. I've lost count of the times a player's been suddenly written up as an England candidate when, to my mind, he's just not international class. I've got no axe to grind about anyone, because I'm not part of the Test scene, but I think I know something about the game and I believe there've been some funny selections in my time in England. Several players who turn out for fashionable counties in the London area have been lucky to play for England so often, while men like Alan Jones of Glamorgan, Geoff Cook of Northants and (for a long time) David Steele never got anywhere near selection. To my mind, performances in county cricket should be a relevant guide to Test selection, yet David Gower gets back into the England team for the showpiece Centenary Test, even though he hadn't really made all that many runs for Leicestershire. The press have always raved about Gower and I think he's a fine player, probably the most naturally talented batsman England have had in my time, but I think he's played more often for England than he's deserved, because he hasn't put in the performances at county level. Robin Jackman did just that and yet it got him nowhere. In 1980 he took more wickets in first-class cricket than any other bowler since 1971, yet he not only failed to get into the Centenary Test, but he also missed out on the England trip to the West Indies. I'm convinced he didn't make it because the press kept going on about the fact that he was too old at thirty-five. But unlike some of the other younger English bowlers chosen for that trip,

Jackman isn't injury-prone and he could be excused for wondering just what he has to do to play for his country. It also seemed strange to me that the press didn't pick up the fact that Brian Rose of Somerset failed to make the England side for the 1980 Centenary Test. Officially he wasn't fit – yet he played a John Player game against us a few days before the Test, and during the Test he turned out for Somerset! That was a much more interesting story than Botham's waistline!

Fleet Street helped to get Ian Botham the England captain's job by a sustained campaign reminiscent of the one launched in 1975 to get Tony Greig the job – the one about the young, dashing all-rounder blowing the cobwebs away from English cricket by leading from the front, etc. I believe the press should have concentrated more on Botham being groomed for the job, rather than expecting him to be suitable for it immediately. Then they became obsessed with his weight problems, even down to asking his wife what she cooks for him, instead of attending to the more urgent problem of getting him some tactical help and guidance for the difficult task he faced.

I suppose it's human nature that the England selectors would like to be praised by the press. Nobody likes picking up a paper and being told you're not doing your job properly, even though your credentials for the task are far superior to those of your critic. But it's common knowledge on the county circuit that the press help to pick the England team, and I doubt if that will ever change.

12

Money and Cricket

I was paid 150 Rand when I played in my first Test in 1967. To me that was a bonus, because I'd have paid to represent my country. From that time onwards, I just played the game and didn't give much thought to money. I negotiated a satisfactory contract with Gloucestershire when I joined them in 1968 and financial considerations remained very low on my list of priorities as I concentrated on learning about cricket.

It was not until 1970 that it dawned on me that there was money to be made out of cricket. I was playing for Western Province and coaching at Stellenbosch University for a nominal sum when I got a telegram at Bristol during the English season. It was from the Rhodesian Cricket Union, offering me a very good contract to play and coach there. I couldn't believe the sum mentioned was correct, it appeared far too high – in fact, I remember going to the bank to check the exchange rate. I was sure there was some mistake but no, they wanted me in Rhodesia for a great deal of cash and as I'd always enjoyed playing in that country I had no hesitation in accepting their offer.

I've never really bartered for money with any of the teams I've played for, but I gradually began to realise that I might have undersold myself. I didn't go round asking

extortionate sums for playing, I just became aware of the
going rate. So when Kerry Packer came along, he found
me very easy to deal with; quite apart from the attraction
of the cricket, the money was just too good to turn down. I
had a wife and two children and a responsibility to them.
Maryna had thrown up a good tennis career to marry me
and raise a family and I was conscious of being the
breadwinner. So I became aware of my commercial
potential – but not in the same way as Barry Richards.
Barry always thought he should get more cash, not only
for playing cricket, but also for the fringe sidelines like
interviews with the media and advertising. It was a great
shame that he allowed himself to be distracted by
financial considerations; he was the greatest batsman of
my generation yet it all became a bore to him. He got sick
and tired of three-day cricket, so Hampshire very kindly
allowed him just to turn out on Sundays in the John
Player League, because they had a good chance of
winning it. But after a couple of weeks, Barry just packed
it all in and left for Australia. I know the Hampshire lads
were all very bitter about Barry's behaviour and I don't
blame them.

Barry always maintained that the top cricketers should
get the same amount of cash as the world's best tennis
players, soccer stars or golfers. I just couldn't see how that
could be justified. Cricket is not a worldwide professional
sport and it's not big business in the way that golf is. A
complex character, Barry, he had moods of depression
and occasional flashes of temper that didn't do his career
any good. There was the time in East London in 1966
when he literally kicked away his chances of playing for
his country that season against the Australians. He'd just
made a glorious hundred against the Aussies at the Jan
Smuts ground and everyone was raving about the innings.
Both teams were invited to a cabaret in a local hotel later
that evening and we all readily accepted. Eventually a

133

group of us turned up a little late at the hotel, only to be told we couldn't come in. Chris Wilkins, Hylton Ackerman and myself gave up trying to persuade the doorman to let us in, but Barry wouldn't let it go. In his frustration, he kicked over a vase which was standing alongside the swimming-pool. That did it – the place was suddenly swarming with bouncers and Barry was hauled into the manager's office. I called Derek Dowling, a South African selector, to try to smooth things over – in retrospect this was a mistake, but one made in good faith, because the alternative was a night in jail for Barry. Derek calmed down the manager but the other selectors got to hear about it. Barry batted number 8 in the second innings of the Aussie match. He played well against them every time he faced the tourists in that season but he never got in the Test side. He had to wait until 1970 for his debut and it remains a tragedy that Barry Richards only played four times for his country. But that night in the East London hotel can't have helped and Barry shouldn't have lost his temper.

I think Barry's main problem was that he didn't have the appropriate stage for his brilliant talents, so he began eating his heart out about the fact that it would all have been more enjoyable for him if he'd shown the same genius in a more lucrative sport. That's never been a worry for me. I've never thought, 'I could have been a millionaire if I'd been a golfer'. I don't see the point of wishing your life away. Cricket will never have a Mark McCormack to sell the game all over the world; Kerry Packer did his bit, but America and Japan are the places where the big sports money is made, and that's where McCormack has concentrated his sports empire. Cricket will only ever be popular in a few major countries in the world, so any analogies with the earning power of a Nicklaus or a Borg are ridiculous. The amount of money Borg earns from advertising alone is unbelievable – he endorses almost seventy products round the world! I've done a bit of advertising on a small scale and it's easy money. All you have to do is pose for the cameras, say the right words when necessary and collect the cash; I've endorsed Brylcreem, beer, lager, orange juice and milk. The photographs raised a few smiles in the dressing-room, though!

I think advertising on a limited scale on a player's equipment should be allowed as soon as possible. In England the subject has been discussed for several years now and I honestly can't see what's wrong with some discreet symbols on various parts of the clothing. We live in an age of sponsorship and it's time to stop being fuddy-duddy about giving some firm a plug. If they're putting money into cricket, they deserve some kind of a mention.

All of us in cricket should be making a bigger effort to sell the game. As captain of Gloucestershire, I feel it's part of my job to publicise the club whenever possible, and that includes playing in charity matches for nothing, and posing for photographs for the local paper or trade magazine with sponsors. I'm happy to go into the sponsors' tent at close of play and have a chat with them. Their money is helping to run our club and pay my wages and I think all professional players should widen their horizons a little and acknowledge our debt to sponsors.

The game isn't as sentimental as it was, there's a hard financial edge to it now. We're moving into the age of showbiz cricket, where experiments like night cricket and single-wicket competitions are being tried to foster interest in the game and raise money at the same time. I've played two single-wicket games against Ian Botham at Bristol and the crowd loved it. The fact that it's not legitimate cricket doesn't matter, because it's filling the ground and the crowds are enthusiastic. Ian and I kept trying to hit the ball out of sight, the fielders dived around all over the place and the crowd of 6,000 loved it on both occasions. It only lasted about three hours, I picked up £1,000 each time and it proved to me that there's a vast untapped reservoir of people who prefer to be entertained for a couple of hours, rather than watch proper cricket all day.

It's up to the players and the administrators to find something that appeals to that particular market. Once we get them hooked on 'gimmick cricket', they'll possibly see the enjoyment of official, first-class cricket. That's why I'm a fan of night cricket; I played it for Kerry Packer and it was a tremendous spectacle. We've tried it in South Africa with a fair amount of success (although heavy dew is a problem) and there are plans to stage an inter-state limited-overs league at night. I don't see why the same thing can't catch on in England – to say that the weather would ruin it is just an easy way out. You could choose two nights a week, with the second as a stand-by. It's purely exhibition stuff to please the crowds, so there's no need to worry about having to play forty overs. The administrators should forget about making it as near to the real thing as possible: it's not, it's simply showbiz played on artificial wickets. And it pays; Chelsea Football Club took as much from their night match involving Essex and the West Indies as Gloucestershire did in the whole of the same season. Night cricket can help secure the future of the official brand which throws up the stars who draw the crowds to the floodlit version – these spectators only want to see Test players who come through from first-class cricket. So it's obvious that first-class cricket must be financially cushioned, and any way that can be arranged should be encouraged. The players should turn up to night cricket with smiles on their faces and ensure that the spectators go home in the same frame of mind.

Tradition is one thing, but professionalism is another.

In England, the Test and County Cricket Board realised this in the nick of time and started changing things. I remember the howls of derision from players, press and public when the John Player League was introduced: 'You can't play a proper game of cricket in forty overs, with bowlers coming in off short runs' they said. Well we could and it has now become part and parcel of the game. It's hard work, but it's very competitive (if a little boring tactically). And even more important, it fills the grounds.

But there are still a few financial anomalies in English cricket. I think it is right that a Test player should get a good cash reward for reaching the top of his profession, but to me the amount paid out seems a little out of proportion. The England players got £1,400 per Test against the West Indies and while I think they deserved a fair amount for having to stand up to Messrs Roberts, Holding and Co, that is too much in relation to what other county players receive. There's too big a gulf now between about eighteen cricketers in the England squad and the rest of those eligible for England, some of whom are just as talented as the current internationals. The minimum wage for a capped player in county cricket is now nearly £5,500 a season yet they can get £1,400 for just five days cricket in a Test! I think Cornhill Insurance should provide more money to the counties – who after all, gave the Test players their first chance – rather than to an élite who are lining their pockets.

I believe it is wrong that a club should be in the red while one of its players walks off with a big benefit that year. Take the case of Peter Graves of Sussex. He made £38,000 tax-free, yet his club was near to bankruptcy at the same time. That wasn't the fault of Peter Graves – he'd waited patiently for his benefit and clearly worked hard at it when it was his turn – but the club must always be bigger than the player, and if Sussex went out of business

137

there'd be a hell of a lot of players and administrative staff looking for jobs elsewhere while Peter counted his money. If Peter had been paid more money in the past, his club could have declared a benefit for *itself* and then worked to get out of the red.

I also don't like the system of capping players and seeing their salaries rocket up as a result. I think there's too big a gap between what the capped and the uncapped player earns: I think it's right that the uncapped player should strive to reach official recognition as an important member of the side, but he doesn't get enough money during that formative process. If you're under twenty and uncapped, you earn less than £3,000 in county cricket and how far does that go? Yet his salary goes up by £2,000 if he gets a cap during the season. When I first captained Gloucestershire, I made a point of 'capping' as many players as possible, because I thought they were not getting enough money for all the great work they were doing for me. Now that wages for capped players are at last going up, I'm sure I'd face a harder fight from the club about capping so many players because it would add a lot to the annual wage bill. I can see the time when one or two experienced players get the sack before they qualify for a benefit, because a club can get two uncapped players for the price of one older pro, who's still got a lot to offer.

But it's better to let a young player go if it's clear he's not going to make it, rather than let him hang around at the club till he's too old to try anything else. That was the situation with Jim Foat at Gloucestershire; now Jim had been in the first team for some time, and although a brilliant fielder, he'd never really established himself as a batsman. I always felt he had more ability than people realised and I pressed for his cap, because I thought he would then relax and do himself justice. We capped him in June, after he'd scored a good hundred against Hampshire, but his form didn't really pick up after that. In the

end we decided he wasn't going to get any better and we
sacked him at the end of the season. The club was
criticised in some quarters for insensitivity, but I felt that
was unfair. We'd encouraged Jim to believe in himself,
but eventually he didn't make the grade. With the
minimum wage now established in county cricket (and not
before time), I can see a lot more Jim Foats suffering the
same fate, because the counties will say they just can't
afford to keep borderline players for another season, due
to the soaring wages bill. Cricket will get more and more
like a branch of industry.

Cricket is now a business and committee men should
divorce themselves from trying to run things on the field
and concentrate instead on raising money for the club. I
know of only a handful of administrators who run cricket
in a businesslike manner. Ken Graveney, Gloucestershire's chairman, is one and Mike Turner at Leicester is
another. Ken was one of those who helped the club secure
its future by selling its ground to an insurance company
and we're now on a far better financial footing than when
I first came over. Ken is a businessman and he has
approached his job in a thoroughly businesslike fashion;
he played for Gloucestershire (indeed he once took all ten
wickets for them in a county match) but he never tries to
tell me how to run the playing side of the club unless I
approach him for advice.

I think cricket managers should also help with the
smooth running of a county side and free those committee
members best qualified for the task of fund-raising. I
admit I used to think that a cricket manager was a
gimmick but now I can see the point; an experienced
former player can take a lot of responsibility off the
shoulders of the captain by attending to all the minute
details that are often too much for one man. Sometimes I
come to the ground determined to have a word with a

certain player before the game starts – either of encouragement or criticism. But sometimes too many things crop up and I've missed the opportunity. A cricket manager could help in that respect and the two men could virtually make all the cricket decisions at the club. Then the people who sit on the cricket committee could use their expertise and contacts to sell the club to the public, while the captain and manager look after things on the field without interference. And judging by the recent experiences of Warwickshire, Nottinghamshire and Surrey, cricket managers are bringing success to the club. There should, of course, be proper liaison between manager and captain based on mutual respect, and if the club is lucky enough to have committee members with playing experience of county cricket so much the better.

Cricket is just one of many leisure industries competing for the attention of the public. It mustn't sit back and assume the vast goodwill for the game will be enough. All avenues for boosting the coffers of cricket must be explored and the cobwebs of administration swept away. It seems to take years for clear-cut decisions to be made by those who run cricket. While the hierarchy dithered about paying reasonable Test fees, Kerry Packer stepped in and capitalised on the revived public interest in the game and the Establishment's seeming indifference to the players' needs in an increasingly competitive world. And he cut through red tape. At Sydney on the first night of floodlit cricket, huge crowds were gathering at the turnstiles at about seven o'clock in the evening. The gatemen just couldn't cope with 40,000 jostling people. Packer heard about the commotion and walked through the turnstiles to say, 'Let them all in for free, if they can find a seat.' Shrewd public relations, that gesture – would the gentlemen at Lord's have acted so promptly?

Decisions take such a long time to come out of Lord's: there should be a committee able to take executive action in the interests of cricket. Men like Mike Brearley, Ray Illingworth, Peter May, Mike Turner, Ken Graveney and Raman Subba Row could take far-reaching decisions based on their great practical knowledge of the game without getting bogged down by red tape and endless committee discussions.

13

The Fun of Cricket

I've always played it hard on the professional cricket field, but I've never lost sight of the fact that there's a lot of fun to be had when play is over. I've never been one for great introspection and self-analysis when the game is finished, even though I'll talk cricket till all hours if necessary. One of the great assets of English county cricket is the fact that you can make so many friendships up and down the country over the years. Cricketers may be more serious on the field than they used to be, but I've come to know a lot of characters when the game is finished. They may have been hell-raisers and wild party-goers or deadpan practical jokers or even guys totally wrapped up in their own selves ... but they were all characters in their own right.

The most remarkable character I have known in cricket was David Green, the former opening batsman for Gloucestershire. If ever there was a larger-than-life guy, it was Greeny: extremely intelligent and witty, he had an old-fashioned attitude to new-fangled things such as training and fitness programmes. Quite simply, he didn't believe in them. For him, cricket was a way of making a lot of friends, knocking the cover off the ball if possible and making regular attempts to boost the profits of certain breweries. I first met him in 1968; he'd just got the sack from Lancashire, one of the reasons being that he liked a drink and it was felt his performances had been affected. He and I hit it off straight away and at the start of the season we went down the River Avon on a trip arranged by the club so that the committee could get to know the players better. Anyway, Greeny didn't fancy that too much, so he said to me, 'Let's have a few drinks.' Never averse to a challenge, I agreed and we downed five pints of Black and Tan without undue difficulty. This impressed Green and he decided to up the tempo by drinking neat gin. I drank gin and coke and kept up with him in terms of quantity until he was carried off the boat totally unconscious. This was the man who'd just been sacked by Lancashire for drinking! He didn't say a single word that night to the committee members of his new county and I thought to myself, 'We're going to have some fun with this bloke!'

And we did. He and I roomed together whenever we played away games and in that first season we had some great times, along with our captain, Arthur Milton. Now quite a few players had told me Arthur was a bit po-faced and he didn't enjoy the game all that much, but I hit things off with him right from the start. The three of us always seemed the last to go to bed on those away trips. I particularly remember one match that season where the indestructible physiques of Green and Milton were really put to the test. It was at Hove and, with the help of a friendly night porter, we drank till four in the morning; by this time, none of us could literally speak and it was funny to watch Greeny's face. He would think of something typically witty to say, but the words just refused to come out of his mouth! Eventually, Green tired of his inadequacies, called the night porter to get him some paper and a pen and proceeded to write down four pages of Shakespeare! Anyway, later that morning, Green had to open the batting with Milton after we'd been put into bat by Sussex. They put on 315 for the first wicket – a county record – and if you'd seen the state of those two earlier that morning, you just wouldn't believe it possible. Green scored 233 and I was batting with him at the end, trying to calm him down, because he could have got nearer to 400 if he'd felt like it. As far as Green was concerned, it was the end of a perfect day when he put one over on the Sussex captain, Mike Griffith, the son of the former MCC secretary Billy Griffith. Mike was looking a bit doleful at the end of the day, his first as Sussex captain, following the resignation of Jim Parks. So Greeny said to him, 'You know, Mike, I remember someone else making the same balls-up as you by putting the opposition in, and it was also his first day as captain.' Mike said, 'Who was that?' – to be met with the devastating reply, 'Your bloody father!' I've no idea if this was true, but Greeny had this enviable knack of sounding knowledgeable and he could bluff his way through anything. I suppose his Oxford University education made him sound even more impressive, but he was certainly a superb deadpan leg-puller.

I lost count of the times David Green set me up during those happy, early days at Gloucestershire. He quickly realised I became very involved and caught up with the emotion of things on the cricket field: a typical South African attitude, I suppose. To someone of Green's detachment and sardonic sense of humour, I must have been a godsend on dull days. There was the time at Hove when he and Kenny Suttle really got me going; I was still pretty quick in those days and, with the Hove wicket encouraging me with a fair amount of bounce, I was roaring in off my full thirty-five-yard run. Unknown to me, Ken said to Green, 'I bet he'd be a bit sick if I pulled away from my guard when he was halfway through his run up.' Green, who was fielding at short leg, thought of an even better scheme: to wait till I was at the top of my leap to deliver the ball before backing away. Kenny did just that and shouted, 'Sorry, Mike, I've got a fly in my eye,' just as I was about to deliver the ball; I believed him, especially when I saw Greeny dabbing Kenny's eye with a handkerchief. Little did I know they were tears of mirth he was dabbing! Anyway, Kenny did it to me three times in a row, which got me mad, because I'd run a hell of a long way without even getting to deliver the damned ball. Finally, I rumbled their scheme, realised that the snigger- ing, bulky figure of Green at short leg was behind it all and when I finally managed to deliver the ball, I deliberately bowled a wide – very close to Green's nose. Honours even.

But he got the better of me once with a devastating quip. It was at Chesterfield, a place where there's not all that much to do; the usual trio of Green, Milton and Procter were trying to think of ways to pass the time in our hotel, and we settled on a game of darts. I decided the traditional game of 301 was a little boring, so I introduced them to 'killer darts', a variation on the theme that's very popular in South Africa. Unfortunately I couldn't quite remember the rules, apart from the fact that you had to go round the board. I wasn't going to let on, though, to my partners and kept saying, 'Just get on and play' when they raised objections that there seemed no way of ending the game under the rules slurringly outlined by me. After about forty-five minutes, we'd made little or no progress and I had to admit that I might possibly have got it all wrong. Came the retort, 'It's a golden rule in cricket that you never find brains combine with pace!'

In that first season of 1968, before the John Player League started, we often had Sundays to ourselves and Green and I found ways to pass the time happily. One particular Sunday found us both the worse for wear after a fairly heavy Saturday night at a function in Coventry for Tom Cartwright's benefit. We decided that 'the hair of the dog' was the best method of improving our Sunday morning malaise, so we adjourned to a nearby hostelry as soon as they opened. After a few beers, we discovered we were both interested in rugby; at that time South Africa was top of the heap in international circles and I lost no time in ramming that fact down the Englishman's throat. Not to be outdone, Greeny suggested that this only applied to internationals, and that he was a far better rugby player than M. J. Procter. Well, I've never ducked a challenge like that, and one glance at the bulky form of Green convinced me that my eminence as the former fly-half of Natal Schoolboys would surely carry the day. After all it took Greeny all his time to stop a cricket ball, especially off my bowling. But he started bragging about his abilities as a forward, about all the crashing tries he'd scored, all the subtle changes of pace, etc, etc. This got too much for me, so I challenged him to a single-wicket rugby match.

Back at the hotel, we paced out an area seventy yards long and twenty wide on the lawn and agreed that each would try to run past the other without putting a foot in touch. I won the toss and after we'd taken off our suit jackets, I asked Green to take first crack. As I waited for him, I assumed he would try something cunning like a side-step. Not a bit of it – he ran straight at me and bowled me over. I recovered just in time to grab his shoe as he hurtled past me. I hung on grimly, he couldn't escape, so the score was still 0 – 0. That remained the score for the next forty-five minutes, as we ran at each other, lumbered into tackles and proved totally incapable of evasion. The beer started working on us and eventually we slumped exhausted on the lawn, cursing the grass stains on our suit trousers. Just then our senior pro, John Mortimore, turned up and enquired whether we'd forgotten about the county match against Warwickshire that we were due to resume on the following day. But all's well ... we bowled them out the next day on a dodgy wicket.

But to this day, Green maintains he's the better rugby player.

I'll never forget the time he ended up in jail for the night in Birmingham – the famous Green turn of phrase was absent that night. Tony Brown and the two of us had gone for a few drinks to a club in the city centre, and I was leaning on a guy's car outside the club, waiting for the other two before leaving. All of a sudden the car owner came up and asked me what the hell I was doing with his car. I replied suitably and the next thing I knew a punch had whistled past my ear. I threw one back, Green and Brown turned up to help, and all of a sudden we were surrounded by about fifty tough-looking characters. We never stood a chance, and it was a frightening experience. I ended up having stitches in hospital and for some reason, Green was thrown in jail. The next day, the three of us turned up to play Warwickshire at Edgbaston, looking distinctly rough. Our secretary, Graham Parker, went over to the press box, explained why three of his players had stitches and black eyes and asked the press boys to keep it out of the papers. They did so and nobody knew a thing about it until a sports reporter in Bristol picked up the story. When we got back to Bristol, it was all over the local paper. That took a bit of explaining, even though we were totally innocent.

Whenever I think of David Green, I think of the fun we had together. He just lived for the hell of it all, and I wish there were more like him around today. The game has become more serious because there are more competitions and therefore extra cash to be won. He was a fine player too – a front foot batsman, who gave the ball a tremendous crack. He made over 2,000 runs in his first season at Gloucestershire and he was my kind of cricketer; he'd crack the first ball of the match for six if he could. He went out of the game at the age of thirty-two, which was a tragedy for the spectators and his many friends. I suspect he'd realised how the professional game was going to develop and he didn't fancy all the training, etc. He should have gone further in the game but perhaps if he'd been more committed, he wouldn't have been such fun.

One of the greatest leg-pullers I've known in the game was 'Tiger' Lance, the South African all-rounder. In 1966 he set up a practical joke that in retrospect was amazingly reckless. We were flying back from Rhodesia to Johannesburg after playing in a match to celebrate the seventy-fifth anniversary of the Salisbury Cricket Club. There were the usual high spirits on the flight back and, unknown to us, Lance had concocted a devilish plan. He enlisted the willing support of Ray White, the Transvaal and Gloucestershire batsman. They somehow managed to steal the customs forms that we'd already filled in – then they added some information. Chris Wilkins' form declared that he had flick-knives and other offensive weapons to declare, Barry Richards apparently had ten ounces of marijuana while mine revealed that I had 'a Luger and ten rounds of ammunition'! We never bothered looking at our forms as we handed them over at Johannesburg Airport and we couldn't work out what all the fuss was about as we were marched off for interrogation. We missed our connection back to Durban and we took a lot of flak from our parents. Afterwards, Tiger and Ray admitted the joke had gone too far – a fortnight after the Prime Minister's assassination is never the best time to make jokes like that.

Tiger had a great line in witty one-liners. Once he was playing on a country ground a hundred miles from Johannesburg. He was then a regular member of the Test side and, as such, a bit of a personality in this match. A young spinner was bowling so well that his captain had to take him off in case the game was over too early and the match was spoiled for the spectators. Tiger was standing in the gully when the spin bowler came to stand in the slips, a little cheesed off because he'd been relieved of his successful duties with the ball. Tiger said, 'Well bowled – you must be the best spinner in the country.' This bucked up the youngster and he thanked Tiger for those few kind words. Came the reply, 'But it's a pity you're not so good in the towns.'

I managed a similar deadpan ruse once on Frank Twistleton, the former chairman of Gloucestershire. Frank was in charge of an International Wanderers tour of Rhodesia and South Africa and they came to play at Salisbury. I was captain of the Rhodesian team and in the bar one night, and I set up a guy to pose as a gangster. I told him to frighten the life out of Frank and he did just that. He was one of the roughest-looking blokes I've ever seen and his performance was superbly realistic. He poked Frank in the chest and said, 'You're the manager of our opposition team and I'm going to show you the night-life of Salisbury. You'll be OK with me and the gang,' and looking at his Mafia-style moustache and scarred face, there was no doubt about the kind of gang he meant. I had a quiet word with Frank. 'You'd better watch out, he's one of the biggest gangsters in Rhodesia. He was shut up in a gang fight in London, nobody argues with him.' By this time, poor old Frank was in a right state and he went off and told my friend with the droopy moustache that he'd be delighted to sample the night-life with him and that he was only joking about going to bed. But Frank, a resourceful man, organised his escape with the help of Brian Davison. As soon as the tough guy's back was turned, Davison tapped Frank on the shoulder and he bolted for the door. He then locked his bedroom door and refused to open it to anybody. The next day at the ground, I told Frank how mad the gangster had been because he'd been insulted and that he was coming to see him later that day. Frank didn't relax until his plane left Salisbury. I think he still believes I was mixed up with gangsters in my time in Rhodesia.

So many laughs, so many characters. One of the funniest trips I've had was to Ireland. Now I know everyone tells Irish jokes and we all enjoy suggestions that the Irish are not the sharpest people in the world. Over in South Africa, we have the same sort of affectionate jokes about the Van Der Merwes. I didn't really believe that the Irish were all that different from anybody else until I went over there with my benefit organiser, David Drinkwater. We were due to meet up with Gary Player to organise a golf tournament as part of my fund-raising activities in the following summer. The whole trip was unbelievable, a laugh from start to finish. When we flew into Ireland, the car we had booked turned out to be an ancient old crate with hardly any gears and just about enough power to get to the top of the nearest hill. We were only about three miles from the course where Gary was competing, so we set off in our bone-shaker and we soon got lost. We asked this guy how we could get to the golf course and his instructions were mind-blowing. He seemed to know what he was talking about until after about five minutes of utter confusion, he stopped and said, 'No, cancel all that – I'll try again, because that'll send you in the opposite direction.'

Eventually we unravelled his mind and we got to the golf course. Gary was out on the course so we decided to savour the delights of their beer tent. It was a huge long bar and I was impressed with the warm welcome we were given and the long list of lagers available. There were about thirty of them on the list, but every time I asked for one of them I was told by a smiling barman, 'Sorry, sir – we don't have that one available today.' Finally, I'd worked my way through the whole list and not one of them was on offer – finally in desperation I said, 'I'll have stout then,' and was told, 'Ah yes, sir, we've got plenty of that – which kind of Guinness would you like?'

On our way back to the airport a few days later, we stopped at a pub to sample some more of the warm Irish hospitality. The pub was all locked up, even though there were about five cars parked outside. We hung around for about ten minutes, then David and I decided to look round the back. We walked through the kitchen and finally stumbled across about ten people having a drink and a chat. We were welcomed very warmly and we sat down and joined them. We asked why the pub wasn't open and we were told, 'The barman's gone on holiday with the keys to the front door.' So the only way to get a drink in that pub was a route march round the back through the kitchen.

I haven't laughed so much or shaken my head in disbelief so many times in such a short time. Ireland's a fantastic place, the people are so generous, warm-hearted and unconsciously funny. But a sense of humour is a vital asset on a trip to that beautiful country!

There's a great deal of fun to be had playing cricket at any level. It's the kind of game that lends itself to humorous incidents and characters. I've always known how lucky I've been to be a professional cricketer; how many people can honestly say they get paid to do something they really enjoy? That's why I am happy to turn out in charity matches or games against club cricketers. Some of my fellow-professionals look down on these matches as being unworthy of their talents, but as far as I'm concerned, these are relaxing and enjoyable occasions. In England, club cricket is the life-blood of the game; many players graduate to county cricket from it and we have a duty to foster interest by showing up to play with them. I feel the same way about the matches we play in Bristol to boost the funds of the Hospital Broadcasting Service. They do a fantastic job for those unlucky enough to be stuck in a hospital bed and I like to think that the rest of the Gloucestershire players are as happy as I am to give up some time a couple of times a year to raise money for the radio people.

It's hard work playing cricket all the year round, but that just doubles the chance of enjoyment if you've got the right attitude to the game and know when to relax from its cares. And I've had plenty of opportunities to do just that. There were, for example, the riotous parties with Hylton Ackerman in my early days, when we shared a flat on the beachfront at Durban. Those parties became something of a legend in Durban at the time and it was just as well for my cricketing career that I got them out of my system early, married young and stabilised my homelife. Hylton Ackerman and I also had some great times together on the South African Schools tour to England in 1963.

I've had some great moments with my old friend, David Drinkwater, a man who loves his cricket and the fun that goes with it; there was the time in Rhodesia when we had been to a party and shared the driving, with me on the brakes and David doing the steering. I swear I've never driven better! I remember bowling a chocolate cake at him in a village match, which prompted the local paper headline, 'Procter Finds Drinkwater's Batting a Piece of Cake'! Then there was the time when Norman Featherstone added his own whimsical comment to the fact that playing for Middlesex doesn't do you any harm in the eyes of the England selectors: Norman, a Rhodesian, strode to the wicket wearing an England cap and declared, 'All the rest of our team have got one now, why should I miss out?'

I've been lucky to keep going for so long in this game, while still achieving a reasonable level of performances. Apart from training hard when necessary, I think one of the reasons for my continuing enthusiasm for professional cricket is the sheer enjoyment I've had from the many friendships I've made throughout the world. It's true that most of my friends in the game – David Green, Arthur Milton, Hylton Ackerman, Robin Jackman, Brian Davison, to name just a few – have shared my liking for a beer but it has not just been the social side of the game that has attracted me. Anyone who saw the way the South Africans integrated so well with the West Indians in that 1970 Rest of the World side, even down to having a big, successful team bet on the horses under the encouragement of that inveterate tipster Gary Sobers, will admit that cricket breaks down barriers. When left to themselves, cricketers of any age, colour or creed can overcome the obstacles put in their way. I'm sure that will always remain the case, no matter how hard the game is played.

Appendix

Facts and Figures of Mike Procter's Playing Career

compiled by Robert Brooke

Key
Ms = number of matches
Inn = number of innings
NO = number of times not out
HS = highest score
C = number of centuries
F = number of fifties
D = number of ducks
Ct = number of catches
Mdns = number of maiden overs bowled
5 = number of times 5 wickets in an innings
10 = number of times 10 wickets in a match
B/B = best bowling analysis in one innings

Teams played for
In England: Gloucs every season, plus Rest of World
XI in 1970. All first-class cricket abroad played in
South Africa. Regular teams played for in South Africa
as follows: 1965/66–1968/69 Natal; 1969/70 Western
Province; 1970/71–1975/76 Rhodesia; 1976/77–present
Natal.

155

Season-by-Season Record in First-class Cricket

Season	Ms	Inn	NO	Runs	HS	Av'ge	C	F	D
1965	1	1	0	69	69	–	–	–	–
1965/66	7	10	2	410	129	51.25	1	4	1
1966/67	9	13	0	208	51	16.00	–	1	2
1967/68	6	10	1	338	84	37.56	–	3	–
1968	24	40	1	1167	134	29.92	3	6	7
1968/69	8	13	1	182	42	15.17	–	–	–
1969	25	39	4	562	52	16.06	–	2	5
1969/70	9	15	1	532	155	38.00	2	–	–
1970	20	33	7	934	115	35.92	1	5	1
1970/71	8	8	0	956	254	119.50	6	–	–
1971	24	43	4	1786	167	45.79	7	6	2
1971/72	10	19	2	695	107	40.88	1	5	2
1972	19	33	3	1219	118	40.63	3	7	1
1972/73	11	20	2	870	131	48.33	2	4	–
1973	18	29	5	1475	152	61.44	6	4	3
1973/74	12	22	1	686	110	32.67	1	5	1
1974	19	33	3	1033	157	34.43	2	6	1
1974/75	2	4	0	161	68	40.25	–	2	–
1975	4	8	0	220	64	27.50	–	3	2
1975/76	8	14	1	468	121*	36·00	1	2	2
1976	21	38	3	1209	131	34·54	1	8	3
1976/77	8	12	1	261	59	23.73	–	3	–
1977	21	33	2	857	115	27.64	2	3	4
1977/78	1	2	0	44	31	22.00	–	–	–
1978	21	36	3	1655	203	50.15	3	7	2
1978/79	2	4	1	86	55*	28.67	–	1	1
1979	21	36	4	1241	122	38.78	3	7	1
1979/80	8	14	0	420	110	30.00	1	1	–
1980	19	33	2	1081	134	34.87	1	7	2
Totals	**366**	**615**	**54**	**20825**	**254**	**37.12**	**47**	**102**	**43**

Ct	Overs	Mdns	Runs	Wts	Av'ge	5	10	B/B
–	6	2	10	0	–	–	–	–
6	163	43	427	17	25.12	–	–	4/19
7	313.1	92	766	49	15.63	1	1	7/25
4	219.5	60	572	29	19.72	3	1	6/37
9	498.5	106	1218	69	17.65	2	–	6/43
5	256	55	744	32	23.25	1	–	5/89
33	639.3	161	1623	108	15.03	6	1	7/65
6	297.2	90	718	45	15.96	1	–	6/73
16	647	181	1398	65	21.51	2	–	6/38
9	209.4	73	435	27	16.11	1	–	5/8
26	535	149	1232	65	18.95	2	–	5/45
8	360.5	96	833	52	16.02	3	1	7/32
13	426.1	106	960	58	16.55	4	1	6/56
21	412.2	112	1049	60	17.48	4	2	9/71
17	269.3	82	684	32	21.38	1	–	6/41
11	439.3	114	1117	47	23.77	–	–	4/42
10	311.3	78	776	47	16.51	1	–	5/29
2	25	6	54	4	13.50	–	–	2/21
10	60.3	8	257	7	36.72	–	–	4/29
3	107.1	19	373	10	37.3p	–	–	4/109
14	635	146	1908	68	28.06	3	–	7/82
7	360.5	94	936	59	15.86	7	2	7/77
17	777.3	226	1967	109	18.05	9	1	7/35
–	22	5	53	4	13.25	–	–	4/53
11	665.2	184	1649	69	23.90	2	–	7/45
1	79	21	211	18	11.72	2	1	6/25
11	574.5	141	1532	81	18.91	7	1	8/30
5	300.4	80	870	45	19.33	2	1	7/29
17	372.1	102	931	51	18.25	3	1	7/16
299	**9985.1**	**2632**	**25303**	**1327**	**19.07**	**67**	**14**	**9/71**

First-class Record in England: Batting and Fielding

1. For Gloucs:

	Ms	Inn	NO	Runs	HS	Av'ge	C	F	D	Ct
v Derby	12	20	1	845	167	44.47	2	3	1	11
v Essex	12	21	0	636	203	30.29	2	1	3	7
v Glamorgan	19	34	3	1080	152	34.84	2	5	4	13
v Hants	23	39	2	1426	147	38.54	4	9	4	21
v Kent	10	18	1	316	58	18.59	–	2	1	9
v Lancs	10	18	1	656	140	38.59	3	1	2	6
v Leics	11	21	1	762	133	38.10	3	2	2	8
v Middx	14	26	1	944	157	37.76	4	3	7	13
v Northants	14	22	4	697	105	38.72	1	5	1	18
v Notts	10	14	0	492	115	35.14	1	2	–	11
v Somerset	21	37	5	1451	118	45.34	3	8	1	14
v Surrey	15	27	7	929	154	46.45	2	4	2	9
v Sussex	17	30	4	944	113*	36.31	1	7	1	8
v Warwicks	14	23	3	792	118	39.60	1	4	1	19
v Worcs	20	30	1	859	108	29.62	2	2	–	16
v Yorks	13	20	1	549	111	28.90	1	3	2	8
v Oxford U.	2	2	0	136	85	68.00	–	2	–	–
v Camb U.	3	3	1	121	73*	60.50	–	1	–	5
v Australia	3	5	0	91	72	18.20	–	1	2	–
v India	2	4	1	106	51	35.33	–	1	–	1
v New Zealand	1	2	1	119	85	–	–	1	–	–
v Pakistan	1	1	0	24	21	12.00	–	–	–	–
v S. Africa	1	1	0	69	69	–	–	1	–	–
v W. Indies	4	7	0	172	97	24.57	–	1	–	5
Totals	**252**	**426**	**38**	**14216**	**203**	**36.64**	**32**	**69**	**34**	**202**

2. For Rest of World XI

	Ms	Inn	NO	Runs	HS	Av'ge	C	F	D	Ct
v England XI	5	9	3	292	62	48.67	–	2	–	2
Total in England	**257**	**435**	**41**	**14508**	**203**	**36.82**	**32**	**71**	**34**	**204**

First-class Record in South Africa: Batting and Fielding

For Natal	43	70	5	1855	129	28.54	2	13	3	31
For W. Province	5	8	0	323	155	40.38	2	–	–	2
For Rhodesia	46	81	6	3662	254	48.83	11	17	5	53
S. Africa	7	10	1	226	48	25.11	–	–	1	4
South	1	1	0	4	4	–	–	–	–	1
S. African XI	5	8	1	196	54	28.00	–	1	–	3
Invitation XI	1	1	0	29	29	–	–	–	–	1
The Rest	1	1	0	22	22	–	–	–	–	–
Total in S. Africa	**109**	**180**	**13**	**6317**	**254**	**37.83**	**15**	**31**	**9**	**95**
Total in all first-class cricket	**366**	**615**	**54**	**20825**	**254**	**37.12**	**47**	**102**	**43**	**299**

First-class Record in England: Bowling

1. For Gloucs

	Overs	Mdns	Runs	Wts	Av'ge	5	10	B/B Inns	B/B Match
v Derby	363	101	793	40	19.83	1	–	6/43	7/64
v Essex	290.3	81	748	47	15.91	2	–	7/45	9/73
v Glamorgan	556.1	139	1507	75	20.09	4	–	6/94	9/91
v Hants	535.2	146	1280	61	20.98	2	–	6/67	8/103
v Kent	226.3	56	657	26	25.27	–	–	4/29	7/105
v Lancs	286.4	76	729	36	20.25	3	–	7/45	8/84
v Leics	288.2	55	877	39	22.49	3	–	7/26	8/149
v Middx	298.2	57	856	25	34.24	1	–	5/89	5/89
v Northants	399.1	97	1024	46	22.26	3	1	6/71	11/117
v Notts	227.5	45	628	28	22.43	1	–	6/81	6/90
v Somerset	512.3	125	1310	67	19.55	2	–	6/35	7/78
v Surrey	330.4	75	893	34	26.26	–	–	4/25	5/47
v Sussex	438.2	101	1115	61	18.28	3	–	5/20	8/60
v Warwicks	298.5	88	704	39	18.05	2	–	6/28	7/43
v Worcs	517.5	151	1149	96	11.96	7	3	8/30	14/76
v Yorks	333.5	96	759	54	14.06	5	1	6/38	10/91
v Oxford U.	56	24	110	6	18.33	–	–	2/26	4/84
v Camb U.	33.2	13	72	5	14.40	–	–	4/11	5/34
v Australia	36	10	104	1	–	–	–	1/36	1/41
v India	51.3	17	113	10	11.30	1	–	7/13	7/41
v N. Zealand	13	5	31	3	10.33	–	–	2/25	3/31
v Pakistan	18	8	45	3	15.00	–	–	3/28	3/45
v S. Africa	6	2	10	0	–	–	–		
v W. Indies	90	22	272	12	22.67	1	–	5/48	5/62
Totals	**6207.4**	**1590**	**15786**	**814**	**19.39**	**41**	**5**	**8/30**	**14/76**

2. For Rest of World XI

	Overs	Mdns	Runs	Wts	Av'ge	5	10	B/B Inns	B/B Match
v England XI	211.1	82	359	15	23.93	1	–	5/46	6/72
Total in England	**6418.5**	**1672**	**16145**	**829**	**19.48**	**42**	**5**	**8/30**	**14/76**

First-class Record in South Africa: Bowling

For S. Africa	252.2	80	616	41	15.02	1	–	6/73	9/103
For Natal	1539.1	403	4111	230	17.87	16	6	7/25	11/79
For W.Province	154.2	40	365	19	19.21	–	–	4/18	7/53
For Rhodesia	1392.5	377	3445	186	18.52	8	3	9/71	10/106
South	13	3	53	1	–	–	–	1/13	1/53
S. African XI	169.4	44	440	16	27.50	–	–	4/89	5/81
Invitation XI	19	9	43	4	10.75	–	–	3/19	4/43
The Rest	26	4	85	1	–	–	–	1/56	1/85
Total	**3566.2**	**960**	**9158**	**498**	**18.39**	**25**	**9**	**9/71**	**11/79**
Total in first-class cricket	**9985.1**	**2632**	**25303**	**1327**	**19.07**	**67**	**14**	**9/71**	**14/76**

First-class Competition Records

County Championship: all for Gloucs

Batting and fielding	Ms	Inn	NO	Runs	HS	Av'ge	C	F	D	Ct
	235	400	35	13378	203	36.65	32	61	32	191

Bowling	Overs	Mdns	Runs	Wts	Av'ge	5	10	B/B Inn	Mtch
	5913.5	1489	15029	774	19.42	39	5	8/30	14/76

Currie Cup

Batting	Ms	Inn	NO	Runs	HS	Av'ge	C	F	D	Ct
Natal	41	67	5	1779	129	28.69	2	13	3	30
W. Province	4	6	0	158	124	26.33	1	–	–	2
Rhodesia	39	68	6	2685	174	43.31	7	13	5	43
Total	**84**	**141**	**11**	**4622**	**174**	**35.55**	**10**	**26**	**8**	**75**

Bowling	Overs	Mdns	Runs	Wts	Av'ge	5	10	B/B Inn	Mtch
Natal	1484.1	387	3963	223	17.77	16	6	7/25	11/79
W. Province	127.2	34	295	17	17.35	–	–	4/18	7/53
Rhodesia	1209	322	3080	162	19.01	8	3	9/71	10/106
Total	**2820.3**	**743**	**7338**	**402**	**18.25**	**24**	**9**	**9/71**	**11/79**

Procter's total of Currie Cup wickets places him second on the all-time list behind VAP van der Bijl. They are the only two with more than 400 Currie Cup wickets.

Test Cricket
For S. Africa: all v Australia

Batting	Ms	Inn	NO	Runs	HS	Av'ge	C	F	D	Ct
	7	10	1	226	48	34.83	–	–	1	4

Bowling	Overs	Mdns	Runs	Wts	Av'ge	5	10	B/B Inn	Mtch
	252.2	80	616	41	15.02	1	–	6/73	9/103

Of Procter's 41 Test dismissals, the victims were as follows:
GD McKenzie, IR Redpath, KR Stackpole each 5;
JW Gleeson, KD Walters, HB Taber each 3;
IM Chappell, WM Lawry, LC Mayne, AP Sheehan, RB Simpson, TR Veivers each 2;
AN Connolly, RM Cowper, AA Mallett, DA Renneburg, GD Watson each 1.

Only one bowler, AN Connolly, dismissed Procter more than once in Test cricket; he did it twice. JW Gleeson, GD McKenzie, AA Mallett, RB Simpson, KR Stackpole, KD Walters and DA Renneburg each dismissed Procter once.

Record at Specific Grounds in First-class Matches

Batting	Ms	Inn	NO	Runs	HS	Av'ge	C	F	D	Ct
Bristol	70	118	12	4189	157	39.52	11	18	9	45
Cheltenham	31	52	6	1708	134*	37.13	5	7	2	36
Gloucester	20	34	3	1357	203	43.77	4	7	2	21
Lord's	8	14	0	289	104	20.64	1	1	6	6
Kingsmead, Durban	26	41	2	1122	129	28.77	2	3	1	16
Police Ground, Salisbury	15	24	2	1227	254	55.77	4	3	1	14
Queen's Club Bulawayo	12	20	3	731	119	43.00	1	6	2	22

| | | | | | | | | | B/B | |
Bowling	Overs	Mdns	Runs	Wts	Av'ge	5	10	Inn	Mtch
Bristol	1766	445	4494	224	20.06	12	–	7/13	8/84
Cheltenham	739	211	1867	109	17.13	6	2	7/16	14/76
Goucester	500.4	137	1202	63	19.08	3	–	6/67	8/60
Lord's	178.1	35	448	12	37.33	–	–	3/21	4/35
Kingsmead	825.5	196	2245	122	18.40	6	2	7/29	10/72
Salisbury	462.3	147	1112	65	17.11	3	1	7/25	11/79
Bulawayo	445.2	138	1058	60	17.63	2	1	9/71	10/120

Centuries in First-class Cricket

129 Natal v Transvaal, Durban 1965/66
101 Gloucs v Hants, Bristol 1968
105 Gloucs v Glamorgan, Cardiff 1968
134 Gloucs v Middlesex, Bristol 1968
124 W. Province v E. Province, Cape Town 1969/70
155 W. Province v Australia, Cape Town 1969/70
115 Gloucs v Lancs, Manchester 1970
119 Rhodesia v Natal B, Bulawayo 1970/71
129 Rhodesia v Transvaal B, Salisbury 1970/71
107 Rhodesia v Orange Free State, Bloemfontein 1970/71
174 Rhodesia v N. E. Transvaal, Pretoria 1970/71
106 Rhodesia v Griqualand West, Kimberley 1970/71
254 Rhodesia v W. Province, Salisbury 1970/71
133 Gloucs v Leics, Leicester 1971
104 Gloucs v Middx, Lord's 1971
100 Gloucs v Somerset, Bristol 1971
115 Gloucs v Notts, Gloucester 1971
111 Gloucs v Yorks, Sheffield 1971
167 Gloucs v Derby, Chesterfield 1971
113 * Gloucs v Sussex, Bristol 1971
107 Rhodesia v N. Transvaal, Pretoria 1971/72
118 Gloucs v Somerset, Bristol 1972
100 Gloucs v Hants, Gloucester 1972
102 Gloucs v Essex, Westcliff 1972
114 ⎫
131 ⎭ Rhodesia v International Wanderers, Salisbury 1972/73
147 Gloucs v Hants, Bristol 1973
102 * Gloucs v Somerset, Taunton 1973
140 Gloucs v Lancs, Manchester 1973
106 * Gloucs v Worcs, Cheltenham 1973
118 Gloucs v Warwicks, Cheltenham 1973
152 Gloucs v Glamorgan, Swansea 1973
110 Rhodesia v Natal, Durban 1973/74
157 Gloucs v Middx, Bristol 1974
102 Gloucs v Leics, Leicester 1974
121 * Rhodesia v E. Province, Port Elizabeth 1975/76
131 Gloucs v Lancs, Bristol 1976
108 Gloucs v Worcs, Cheltenham 1977 (made before lunch, Day 2)
115 Gloucs v Hants, Bristol 1977
203 Gloucs v Essex, Gloucester 1978
122 Gloucs v Derby, Gloucester 1978

154 Gloucs v Surrey, Guildford 1978 (made over 100 before lunch, Day 2)

122 Gloucs v Leics, Bristol 1979 (made over 100 before lunch, Day 2)

102 Gloucs v Surrey, Cheltenham 1979

105 Gloucs v Northants, Bristol 1979

110 Natal v E. Province, Port Elizabeth 1979/80

134* Gloucs v Middx, Cheltenham 1980

Century Partnerships

116–4 with BA Richards for Gloucs v S. Africa, Bristol 1965 (f-c debut)

279–5 with BJ Versfeld for Natal v Transvaal, Durban 1965/66

149–6 with M Bissex for Gloucs v Hants, Bristol 1968

155–3 with CA Milton for Gloucs v Somerset, Taunton 1968

110–4 with DR Shepherd for Gloucs v Leics, Leicester 1968

170–3 with DR Shepherd for Gloucs v Middx, Bristol 1968

120–7 with GP Pfuhl for W. Province v E. Province, Cape Town 1969/70

109–4 with CG Stephens for W. Province v Australia, Cape Town 1969–70

147–5 with E Laughlin for Rhodesia v Natal B, Bulawayo 1970/71

119–5 with E Laughlin for Rhodesia v Transvaal B, Salisbury 1970/71 (consecutive innings)

150–4 with JD McPhun for Rhodesia v Orange Free State, Bloemfontein 1970/71

127–4 with SD Robertson for Rhodesia v N. E. Transvaal, Pretoria 1970/71

121–5 with BF Davison for Rhodesia v N. E. Transvaal, Pretoria 1970/71

105–3 with JD McPhun for Rhodesia v Griqualand W., Kimberley 1970/71

166–6 with HAB Gardiner for Rhodesia v W. Province, Salisbury 1970/71

116–5 with DR Shepherd for Gloucs v Middx, Lord's 1971

115–3 with RB Nicholls for Gloucs v Somerset, Bristol 1971

185–3 with CA Milton for Gloucs v Notts, Gloucester 1971

119–3 with RDV Knight for Gloucs v Notts, Gloucester 1971

114–4 with M Bissex for Gloucs v Yorks, Sheffield 1971

288–3 with CA Milton for Gloucs v Derby, Chesterfield 1971

167–4 with BF Davison for Rhodesia v E. Province, Bulawayo 1971/72

117–5   with JH du Preez for Rhodesia v N. Transvaal, Pretoria
        1971/72
145/4   with SD Robertson for Rhodesia v W. Province, Cape Town
        1971/72
151–4   with DR Shepherd for Gloucs v Somerset, Bristol 1972
100–3* with RDV Knight for Gloucs v Sussex, Gloucester 1972
121–4   with RB Nicholls for Gloucs v Derby, Cheltenham 1972
111–4   with PR Carlstein for Rhodesia v International Wands,
        Bulawayo 1972/73
169–5   with BF Davison for Rhodesia v International Wands, Salis-
        bury 1972/73
132–3   with Sadiq Mohamed for Gloucs v N. Zealand, Bristol 1973
150–3* with Sadiq Mohamed for Gloucs v Surrey, The Oval 1973
129–3   with Sadiq Mohamed for Gloucs v Hants, Bristol 1973
        (last 3 in consecutive matches)
205–5   with DR Shepherd for Gloucs v Lancs, Manchester 1973
109–3   with RDV Knight for Gloucs v Glamorgan, Swansea 1973
110–5   with BL Irvine for S. African XI v DH Robins' XI, Johannes-
        burg 1973/74
130–5   with BF Davison for Rhodesia v N. Transvaal, Pretoria
        1973/74
114–5   with SD Robertson for Rhodesia v Natal, Durban 1973/74
105–6   with AS Brown for Gloucs v Middx, Bristol 1974
108–4   with DR Shepherd for Gloucs v Somerset, Weston 1974
112–3   with RDV Knight for Gloucs v Kent, Cheltenham 1975
152–3   with Zaheer Abbas for Gloucs v Warwicks, Cheltenham 1975
108–3   with Zaheer Abbas for Gloucs v Sussex, Eastbourne 1975
        (last 3 in consecutive matches)
226–3   with SD Robertson for Rhodesia v E. Province, Port Elizabeth
        1975/76 (Rhodesia 3rd wicket record)
174–2   with JG Heron for Rhodesia v E. Province, Port Elizabeth
        1975/76
119–3   with Zaheer Abbas for Gloucs v Yorks, Leeds 1976
128–3   with Sadiq Mohamed for Gloucs v Yorks, Leeds 1976
136–3   with Sadiq Mohamed for Gloucs v Lancs, Bristol 1976
165–3   with Zaheer Abbas for Gloucs v Sussex, Gloucester 1976
132–3   with Zaheer Abbas for Gloucs v Hants, Southampton 1976
105–3   with Zaheer Abbas for Gloucs v Lancs, Manchester 1977
119–4   with Zaheer Abbas for Gloucs v Somerset, Bristol 1977
219–5   with JC Foat for Gloucs v Essex, Gloucester 1978
181–4   with DR Shepherd for Gloucs v Derby, Gloucester 1978
103–5   with JC Foat for Gloucs v Glamorgan, Cardiff 1978
196–4   with AW Stovold for Gloucs v Surrey, Guildford 1978

129-2   with Zaheer Abbas for Gloucs v Northants, Northampton 1979
107-3   with A W Stovold for Gloucs v Somerset, Taunton 1979
135-3   with Sadiq Mohamed for Gloucs v Northants, Bristol 1979
195-4   with CP Wilkins for Natal v E. Province, Port Elizabeth
         1979/80
101-4   with Sadiq Mohamed for Gloucs v Middx, Cheltenham 1980
100-4   with Zaheer Abbas for Gloucs v Glamorgan, Swansea 1980
120-3   with Sadiq Mohamed for Gloucs v Somerset, Bristol 1980

Six Wickets in an Innings in First-class Cricket

20-11-25-7   Natal v Rhodesia, Salisbury 1966/67
23.4-4-76-6   Natal v N. E. Transvaal, Pretoria 1967/68
14-3-37-6   Natal v N. E. Transvaal, Durban 1967/68
28-10-49-6   Natal v E. Province, Durban 1967/68
20.5-6-43-6   Gloucs v Derby, Chesterfield 1968
25.1-10-65-6   Gloucs v Yorks, Middlesbrough 1969
26.5-7-71-6   Gloucs v Northants, Northampton 1969
25-4-65-7   Gloucs v Worcs, Worcester 1969
24-11-73-6   S. Africa v Australia, Port Elizabeth 1969/70
20.3-6-38-6   Gloucs v Yorks, Bradford 1970
16-2-32-7   Rhodesia v Transvaal, Johannesburg 1971/72
22-3-56-6   Gloucs v Yorks, Middlesbrough 1972
36.1-17-71-9   Rhodesia v Transvaal, Bulawayo 1972/73
24-3-67-6   Rhodesia v W. Province, Cape Town 1972/73
20.2-7-41-6   Gloucs v Lancs, Manchester 1973
14.3-4-35-6   Gloucs v Somerset, Taunton 1976
24-6-82-7   Gloucs v Leics, Leicester 1976
14-6-28-6   Gloucs v Warwicks, Birmingham 1976
25.5-2-94-7   Natal v Transvaal, Johannesburg 1976/77
37.2-14-77-7   Natal v E. Province, Port Elizabeth 1976/77
16.2-5-28-6   Natal v W. Province, Cape Town 1976/77
37-16-94-6   Gloucs v Glamorgan, Bristol 1977
17.1-6-45-7   Gloucs v Essex, Southend 1977
18.5-5-35-7 ⎫
20-6-38-6   ⎭   Gloucs v Worcs, Cheltenham 1977
19.4-7-40-6   Gloucs v Warwicks, Bristol 1977
39-11-68-6   Gloucs v Hants, Bristol 1977
19-6-45-7   Gloucs v Lancs, Bristol 1978
12-5-25-6   Natal v W. Province, Cape Town 1978/79
16.4-5-30-8   Gloucs v Worcs, Worcester 1979
34-12-67-6   Gloucs v Hants, Gloucester 1979

26-3-81-6	Gloucs v Notts, Nottingham 1979
15.3-8-13-7	Gloucs v India, Bristol 1979
17.5-5-26-7	Gloucs v Leics, Bristol 1979
36-11-107-6	Gloucs v Yorks, Cheltenham 1979
14-5-29-7	Natal v N. Transvaal, Durban 1979/80
15.5-7-16-7 ⎫ 27.3-9-60-7 ⎭	Gloucs v Worcs, Cheltenham 1980

Ten Wickets in a Match in First-class Cricket

41-15-79-11	Natal v Rhodesia, Salisbury 1966/67
56-21-101-10	Natal v E. Province, Durban 1967/68
43.1-9-117-11	Gloucs v Northants, Northampton 1969
41.4-8-106-10	Rhodesia v Transvaal, Johannesburg 1971/72
36.1-4-91-10	Gloucs v Yorks, Middlesbrough 1972
53.4-21-120-10	Rhodesia v Transvaal, Bulawayo 1972/73
47.2-7-131-10	Rhodesia v W. Province, Cape Town 1972/73
58.2-19-131-10	Natal v E. Province, Port Elizabeth 1976/77
44.2-10-144-10	Natal v Transvaal, Pietermaritzburg 1976/77
38.5-11-73-13	Gloucs v Worcs, Cheltenham 1977
35-10-90-11	Natal v W. Province, Cape Town 1978/79
36.4-11-85-10	Gloucs v Worcs, Worcester 1979
33-11-72-10	Natal v N. Transvaal, Durban 1979/80
43.2-16-76-14	Gloucs v Worcs, Cheltenham 1980

All-round Cricket in First-class Matches
(100 Runs and 6 Wickets)

51 & 102: 3/43 & 5/30:	Gloucs v Essex, Westcliffe 1972, match won
140: 6/41 & 1/72:	Gloucs v Lancs, Manchester 1973, match drawn
70 & 33: 2/40 & 4/76:	Rhodesia v Transvaal, Salisbury 1973/74, match drawn
97 & 4* : 1/15 & 6/28:	Gloucs v Warwicks, Birmingham 1976, match won
108: 7/35 & 6/38:	Gloucs v Worcs, Cheltenham 1977, match won
115 & 57: 6/68 & 0/78:	Gloucs v Hants, Bristol 1977, match lost
122: 3/43 & 3/33:	Gloucs v Derby, Gloucester 1978, match won
39 & 90: 3/67 & 3/72:	Gloucs v Somerset, Bristol 1978, match drawn
33 & 74: 4/35 & 4/40:	Gloucs v Hants, Southampton 1979, match won
122: 0/32 & 7/26:	Gloucs v Leics, Bristol 1979, match won
38 & 105: 2/67 & 4/69:	Gloucs v Northants, Bristol 1979, match won

73 & 35: 7/16 & 7/60:   Gloucs v Worcs, Cheltenham 1980, match
won.

NB Procter is only the third cricketer to perform the outstanding
all-round feat of a century and 10 wickets in the same match for
Gloucs. WG Grace did it on 6 occasions, and CJ Barnett once.
Procter's two such feats were the first for Gloucs since 1938.

Hat-tricks in First-class Matches

v Essex, Westcliff 1972: BE Edmeades, B Ward, KD Boyce (all lbw)
(Procter also hit 51 and 102 in this match)
v Essex, Southend 1977: BR Hardie, KE McEwan, GA Gooch (1
bowled, 2 lbw)
v Leics, Bristol 1979: JC Balderstone, PB Clift, K Shuttleworth (1 ct, 2
lbw)
v Yorks, Cheltenham 1979: RG Lumb, CWJ Athey, JH Hampshire (all
lbw) (Procter is the only bowler to have had two 'all-lbw' hat-tricks
in first-class cricket)

Century and Hat-trick in Same Match

102 v Essex, Westcliff 1972: 122 v Leics, Bristol 1979

No other Gloucestershire player has even achieved this feat once for
the County.

Some Examples of Fast Scoring by MJ Procter
in First-class Cricket

(In order to keep the list within reasonable bounds, only scores over 50,
at 70 runs per hour or more are included – unless over 100 runs scored)

72	in 52 mins:	Gloucs v Australia, Bristol 1968
134	in 120 mins:	Gloucs v Middx, Bristol 1968
155	in 130 mins:	W. Province v Australia, Cape Town 1969/70
		(moved from 100 to 155 in 12 mins)
107	in 80*mins:	Rhodesia v Orange Free State, Bloemfontein
		1970/71 (reached 100* in 72 mins)
104	in 80 mins:	Gloucs v Middx, Lord's 1971
		(reached 100* in 79 mins)
64*	in 50 mins:	Gloucs v Sussex, Gloucester 1972
152	in 140 mins:	Gloucs v Glamorgan, Swansea 1973
64*	in 50 mins:	Gloucs v Sussex, Eastbourne 1975 (50* in 35 mins)
97	in 74 mins:	Gloucs v W. Indies, Bristol 1976
203	in 165 mins:	Gloucs v Essex, Gloucester 1978

154 in 110 mins: Gloucs v Surrey, Guildford 1978
52 in 44 mins: Gloucs v Sussex, Bristol 1979
76*in 54 mins: Gloucs v Northants, Northampton 1979
74 in 52 mins: Gloucs v Hants, Southampton 1979
122 in 104 mins: Gloucs v Leics, Bristol 1979
93 in 46 mins: Gloucs v Somerset, Taunton 1979 (50* in 25 mins)
92 in 35 mins: Gloucs v Warwicks, Bristol 1979 (50* in 21 mins)
105 in 60 mins: Gloucs v Northants, Bristol 1979 (100* in 57 mins)
84 in 48 mins: Gloucs v Somerset, Bristol 1980

Slow Scoring

129 in 404 mins: Natal v Transvaal, Durban 1965/66 (maiden century)

Sixes in an Innings

9 in 155: W. Province v Australia, Cape Town 1969/70
8 in 154: Gloucs v Surrey, Guildford 1978
8 in 93: Gloucs v Somerset, Taunton 1979.

Centuries in Succession

During the 1970/71 season Procter scored his 6 centuries, all for Rhodesia, in successive innings, thus equalling the record held by CB Fry (1901) and DG Bradman (1938/39): Procter's hundreds being scored all for the same team is unique, Fry scoring one of his 6 for The Rest of England, the other five for Sussex, and Bradman scoring one hundred for his own team, the others for S. Australia. PN Kirsten, with four successive centuries in 1976/77, stands second to Procter among S. Africans.

BENSON & HEDGES CUP

Batting	Ms	Inn	NO	Runs	HS	Av'ge	100	50	Ct
	36	36	5	1175	154*	37.90	2	7	9

Bowling	Overs	Mdns	Runs	Wts	Av'ge	B/B
	331.4	67	947	63	15.03	6/13

4 wickets in match in Benson & Hedges Cup
11-0-37-5 v Glamorgan, Swansea 1972
9.2-1-26-5 v Somerset, Taunton 1972
8.5-6-4-4 v Min Cos (West), Amersham 1976

11–5–13–6 v Hants, Southampton 1977
11–2–38–5 v Warwicks, Bristol 1978

50s in Benson & Hedges Cup

154* v   Somerset, Taunton 1972
 56 v   Middx, Lord's 1972
 52* v   Min Cos (West), Amersham 1976
 64 v   Lancs, Manchester 1977
 62 v   Derby, Bristol 1978
115 v   Lancs, Liverpool 1978
 86* v   Glamorgan, Swansea 1979
 82* v   Min Cos (Sth), Bristol 1979
 50 v   Glamorgan, Bristol 1980

Century Partnerships

108–3 with RDV Knight v Middx, Lord's 1972
131–3 with Zaheer Abbas v Lancs, Liverpool 1978
137–3 with Zaheer Abbas v Min Cos (Sth), Bristol 1979

Man-of-the-Match Awards

v Somerset, Taunton 1972: 154*:1 ct: 9.2–1–26–5: Gloucs won
v Min Cos (West), Amersham 1976: 52*: 8.5–6–4–4: Gloucs won
v Lancs, Manchester 1977: 64: 5–1–8–0: Gloucs won
v Hants, Southampton 1977: 8: 11–5–13–6: Gloucs lost
v Min Cos (Sth) Bristol 1979: 82*: 11–5–18–2: Gloucs won.

HAT-TRICK

v Hants, Southampton 1977: BA Richards, TE Jesty, JM Rice (2 lbw, 1 b)

DATSUN SHIELD (Until 1976/77 known as GILLETTE CUP)

Batting	Ms	Inn	NO	Runs	HS	Av'ge	50
	19	17	4	402	96	30.92	1

Bowling	Ct	Overs	Mdns	Runs	Wts	Av'ge	B/B
	8	165.3	47	436	25	17.44	4/18

BEST SCORES

96 Rhodesia v Natal, Salisbury 1970/71
44* Natal v Rhodesia, Salisbury 1976/77
41 Rhodesia v Transvaal, Johannesburg 1971/72

BEST BOWLING
9.1–3–12–3 Natal v E. Province, Johannesburg (final) 1976/77
Given Award for Best Bowling in the final, also Man-of-the-Series
Award
12–4–18–4 Natal v N. Transvaal, Pretoria 1977/78

Performances in Limited-overs Competitions

For Gloucs
GILLETTE CUP 1968–80

Batting	Ms	Inn	NO	Runs	HS	Av'ge	100	50	Ct
	24	24	0	789	107	32.88	2	4	5

Bowling	Overs	Mdns	Runs	Wts	Av'ge	B/B
	241.1	44	655	38	17.24	4/21

4 wickets in match in Gillette Cup 12–5–21–4 v Yorks, Leeds 1976

50s in Gillette Cup
53 v Notts, Nottingham 1968
107 v Sussex, Hove 1971
65 v Lancs, Manchester 1971
101 v Worcs, Worcester 1973
94 v Sussex, Lord's 1973
52 v Surrey, The Oval 1980

Century Partnerships
119–3rd with M Bissex v Sussex, Hove 1971
112–3rd with Zaheer Abbas v Sussex, Hove 1979

Man-of-the-Match Awards
v Sussex, Hove 1971: 107: 10–2–20–3: Gloucs won.
v Worcs, Worcester 1973: 101: 12–2–31–3: Gloucs won.

JOHN PLAYER LEAGUE 1969–1980

Batting	Ms	Inn	NO	Runs	HS	Av'ge	100	50	Ct
	153	144	8	3426	109	25.19	1	18	54

Bowling	Overs	Runs	Wts	Av'ge	4 Inn	B/B	6s
	988.3	3442	169	20.36	8	5/8	39

APPENDIX

50s in John Player League

57	v	Hants, Portsmouth 1971
58	v	Middx, Lord's 1972
52	v	Essex, Moreton-in-Marsh 1972
109*	v	Warwicks, Cheltenham 1972
67	v	Notts, JP Gound, Nottingham 1973
98	v	Somerset, Bristol 1974
51	v	Essex, Chelmsford 1974
50*	v	Leics, Gloucester 1974
		(last 3 in consecutive innings)
79	v	Northants, Bristol 1977
78	v	Notts, Nottingham 1977
59	v	Lancs, Bristol 1977
77*	v	Sussex, Bristol 1978
54	v	Glamorgan, Bristol 1979
69	v	Sussex, Hove 1979
51	v	Essex, Gloucester 1980
58	v	Worcs, Bristol 1980
79	v	Sussex, Moreton-in-Marsh 1980
61	v	Yorks, Hull 1980
57	v	Somerset, Bristol 1980

4 wickets in match in John Player League

8-2-27-4	v	Hants, Portsmouth 1969
8-1-19-4	v	Lancs, Bristol 1969
8-2-10-5	v	Sussex, Arundel 1972
8-2-19-5	v	Essex, Gloucester 1973
8-4-18-4	v	Northants, Noton 1974
8-0-26-4	v	Sussex, Hove 1977
5.5-0-8-5	v	Middx, Gloucester 1977
8-2-22-4	v	Notts, Nottingham 1977

Century Partnerships

158-3*	with Zaheer Abbas v Sussex, Bristol 1978
112-3	with Zaheer Abbas v Sussex, Hove 1979
107-2	with BC Broad v Somerset, Bristol 1980
107-3	with Zaheer Abbas v Worcs, Bristol 1980
104-3	with Sadiq Mohamed v Essex, Gloucester 1980
100-3	with Zaheer Abbas v Yorks, Hull 1980

In 1980 Procter became the second player, after P Willey, to reach 3000 runs and 100 wickets in the John Player League.

Index

174

Du Preez, Jack, 69

East, Ray, 98

Foat, Jim, 105
Forrest, Ian, 106
Fortune, Charles, 15
Fotheringham, Henry, 71
Fry, C. B., 79

Garner, Joel, 42, 43, 115
Gatting, Mike, 103
Gavaskar, Sunil, 57
Gibbs, Lance, 35
Gifford, Norman, 105
Gleeson, John, 29, 30, 32, 83
Goddard, Trevor, 26, 28, 30
Gooch, Graham, 122, 124
Gower, David, 59, 122, 124, 130
Graveney, David, 97, 98, 104
Graveney, Ken, 139, 141
Graveney, Tom, 25, 57, 73, 75,
   124
Graves, Peter, 137, 138
Greenidge, Gordon, 36, 92, 100
Green, David, 90, 142–7, 153
Greig, Tony, 20, 23, 37, 38, 40,
   42–7, 49, 50, 122, 131
Griffith, Mike, 144

Hadlee, Richard, 60
Hall, Wes, 25
Hammond, Wally, 120
Hampshire, John, 80, 90
Hawke, Neil, 26
Hayes, Frank, 60
Hendrick, Mike, 88
Henry, Omar, 14
Higgs, Ken, 25
Hignell Alastair, 98
Hobson, Denys, 49, 71
Holding, Mike, 36, 41, 43, 82, 86,
   137
Hookes, David, 43
Howa, Hassan, 18, 19
Hughes, Kim, 124

Illingworth, Ray, 20, 34, 109, 141
Irvine, Lee, 25, 29–31, 62, 64, 129

Jackman, Robin, 130, 153
Jennings, Ray, 71
Jesty, Trevor, 92
Jones, Alan, 33, 130

Kallicharran, Alvin, 60
Kanhai, Rohan, 25, 34, 36, 59
Khan, Imran, 44
Khan Majid, 42
Kirsten, Peter, 22, 60, 62, 71, 123
Knight, Roger, 101
Knott, Alan, 20, 38
Kourie, Alan, 71

Laird, Bruce, 46
Lamb, Allan, 22, 66, 71, 123
Lance, Tiger, 148, 149
Lawry, Bill, 27, 29, 30, 32, 42
LeRoux, Garth, 44, 45, 46, 71
Lillee, Dennis, 37, 41, 43–5, 83,
   87, 102, 115
Lindsay, Dennis, 15, 22, 26–9
Lloyd, Clive, 11, 34, 36, 53, 59, 60,
   113, 114
Lucas, Keith, 112–14
Lumb, Richard, 93

Maley, John, 42
Mallett, Ashley, 29, 43
Marsh, Rodney, 44
May, Peter, 57
McBride, Willie John, 13
McCosker, Rick, 41
McCormack, Mark, 134
McEwan, Ken, 68
McGlew, Jackie, 62, 66, 96, 108,
   120
McKenzie, Graham, 26, 28, 29,
   30, 34, 86
McLean, Roy, 66
Mendis, Gehan, 115
Milburn, Colin, 90
Milton, Arthur, 59, 80, 122, 143,
   147, 153